JOSEPH DARBY

A Man of Sable Island

R. E. WILSON

LUCKY SPROUT PRESS

Published by Lucky Sprout Press
Bedford, Nova Scotia, Canada.

Copyright © 2020 Rebecca Wilson. All rights reserved.
First Edition.

No part of this publication may be copied, stored in a retrieval system, or transmitted in any form by any means, electronic, mechanical, recording or otherwise, except brief extracts for the purpose of review, and no part of this publication may be sold or hired, without the written permission of the publisher.

For more information, please contact:
editor@luckysproutpress.com

Cover design by Offshoot Creative Consulting
Book design by Silverback Books

Dedicated to all the women who worked and served on Sable Island, but who went unmentioned in the documents left behind. I wish I could have written more about you.

To all the passionate folks at the Friends of Sable Island Society, who made my initial research possible.

To Jessie Rickaby, as always.

TO
HIS EXCELLENCY
Lt General Sir James Kempt G.C.B.
Lt GOVERNOR OF NOVA SCOTIA
&c. &c. &c.
The Honble The Members of His Majestys Council
AND
the Gentlemen of the House of Assembly
OF THIS PROVINCE
By whose Bounty and Benevolence
THIS MOST EXCELLENT ESTABLISHMENT
is supported and preserved
THIS CHART AND DESCRIPTION OF
SABLE ISLAND
Is Dedicated with Great Respect
by Their Most Obedient
and very Humble Servant
JOSEPH DARBY.

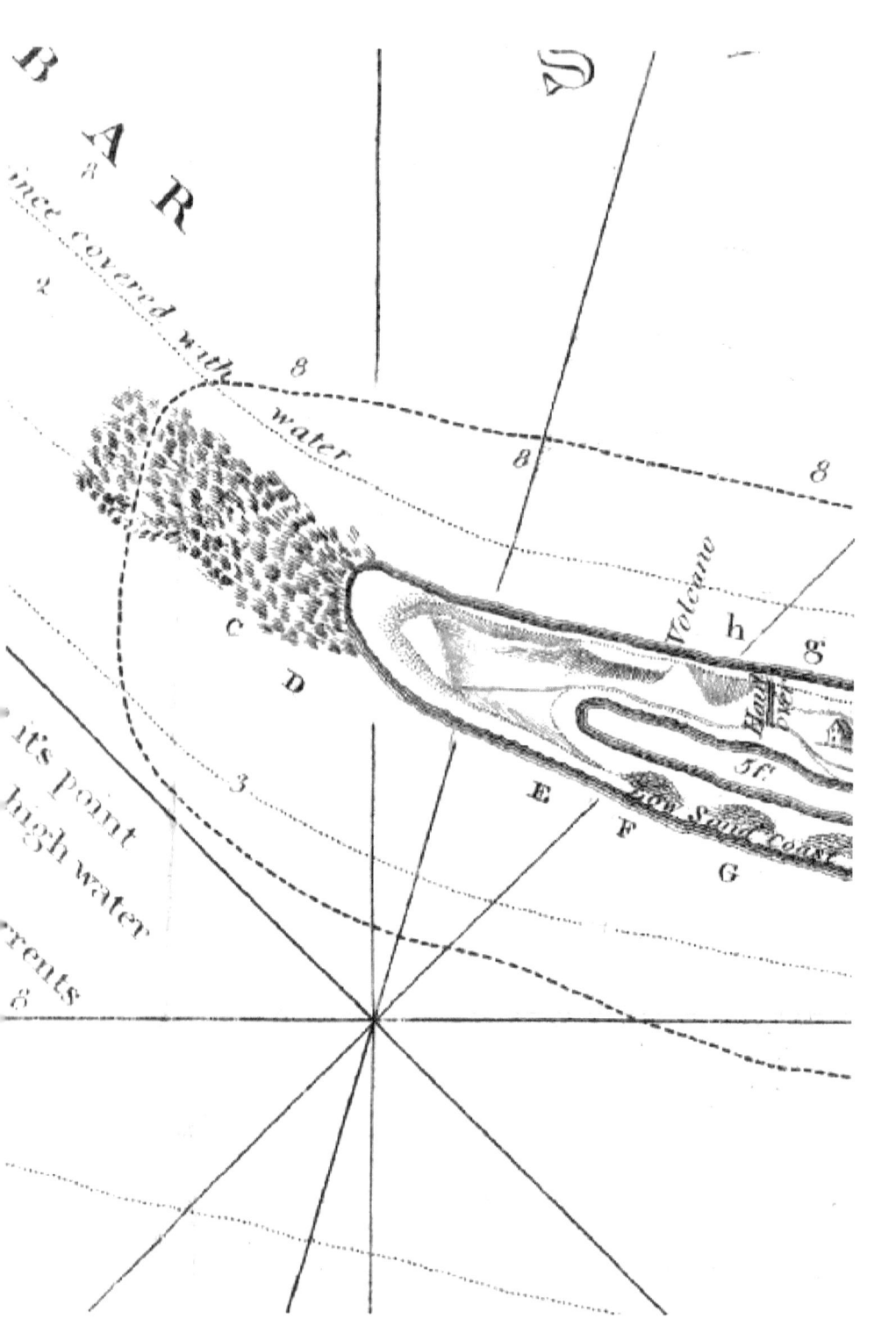

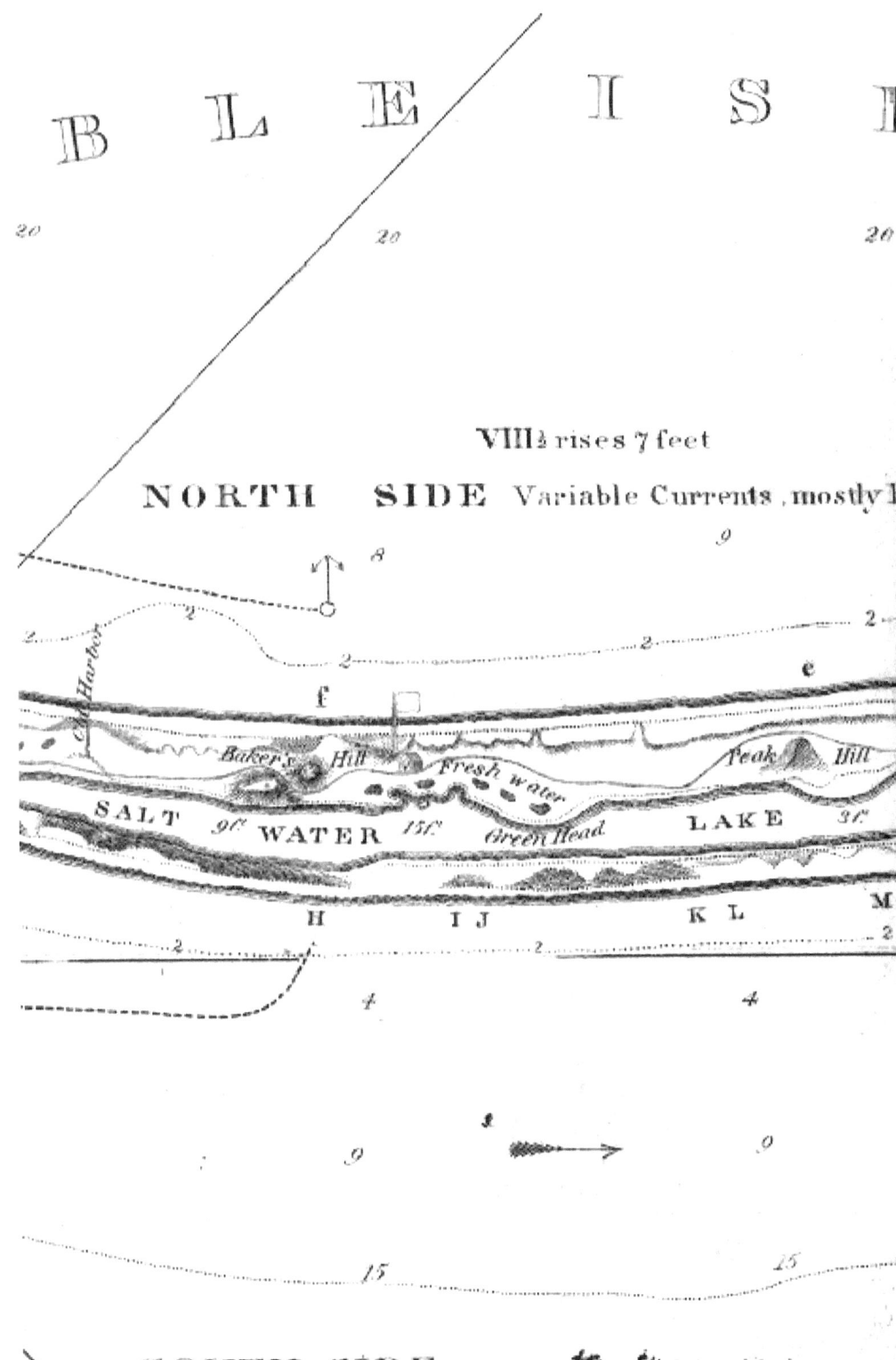

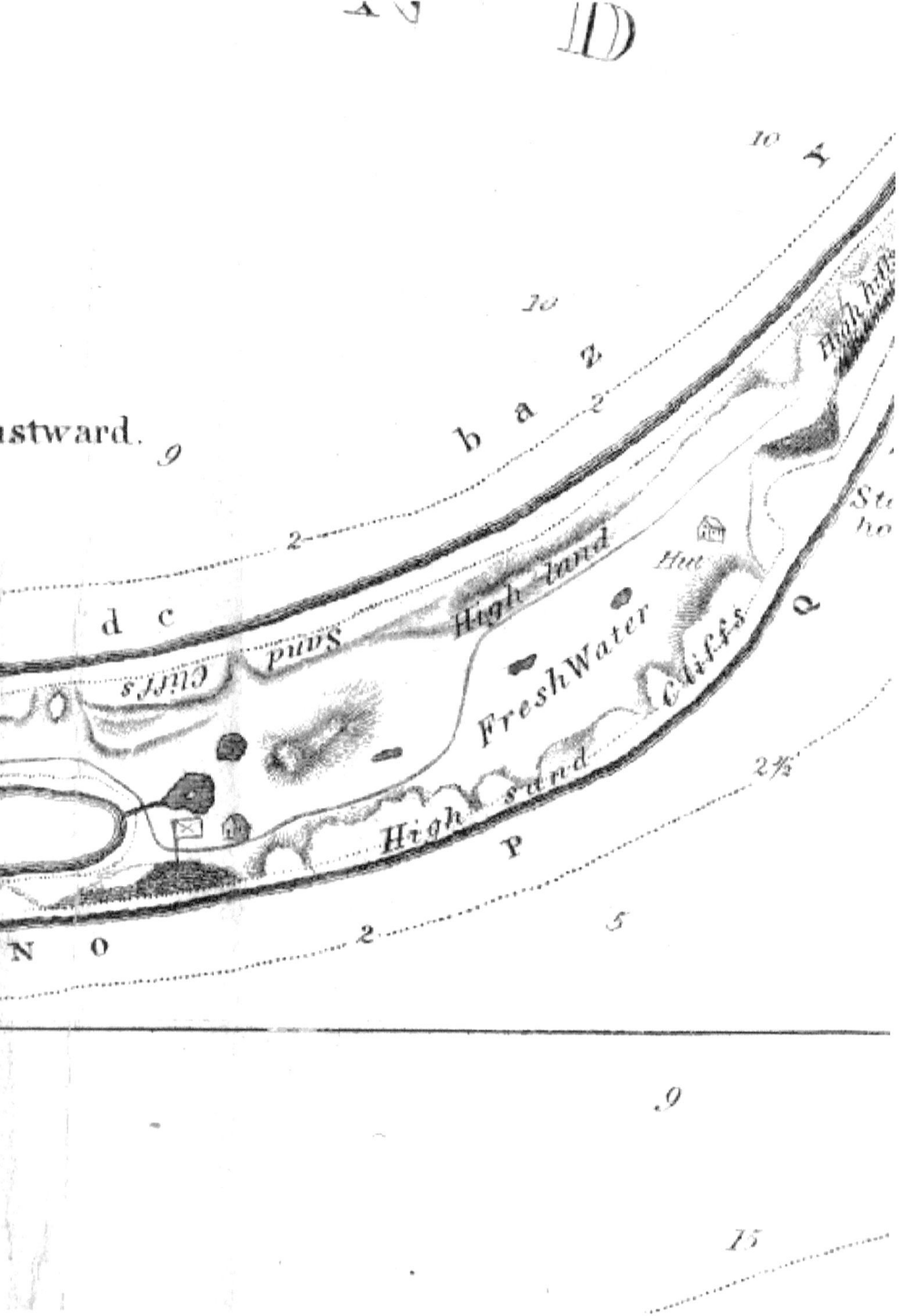

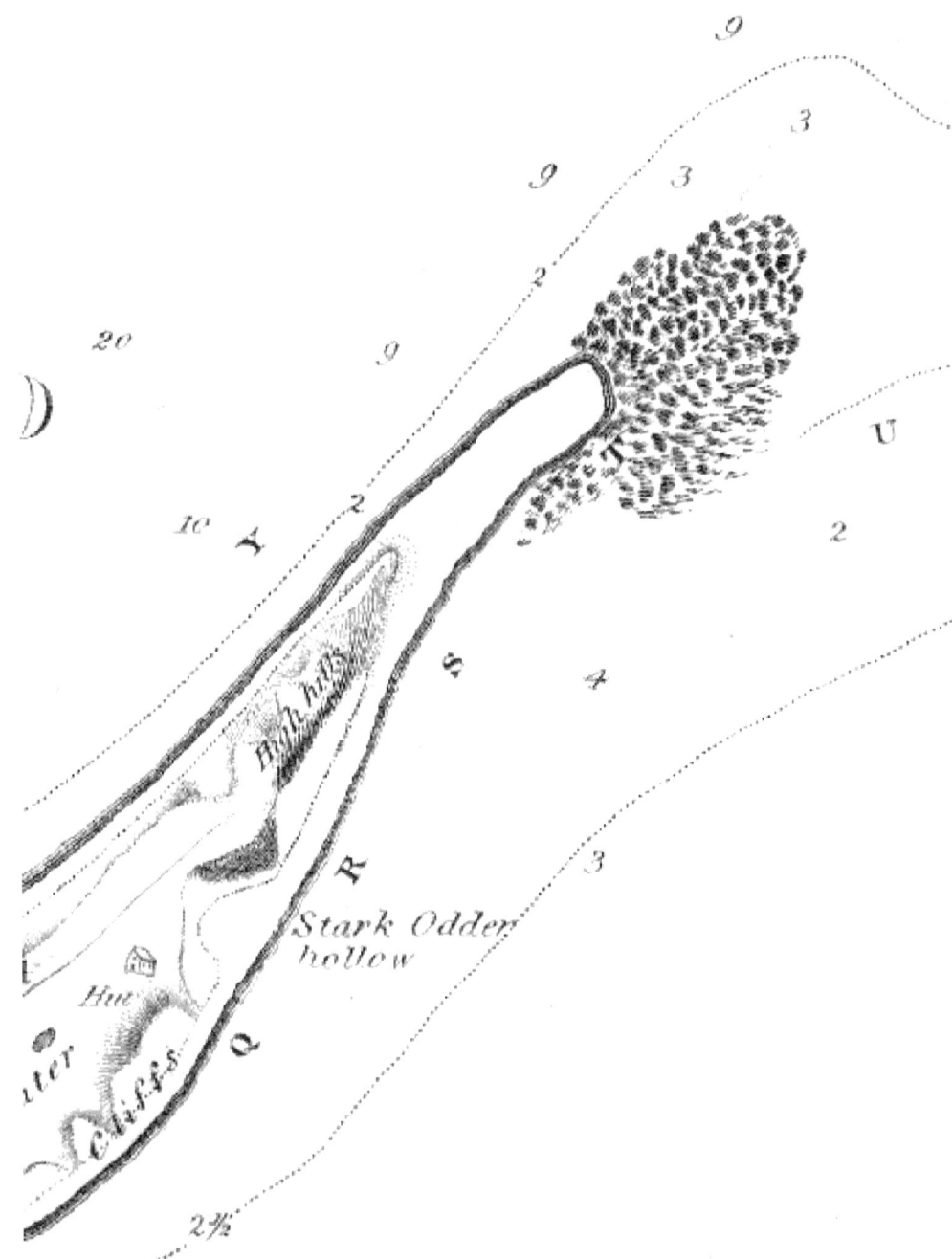

Introduction

My public life is before you; and I know you will believe me when I say, that when I sit down in solitude to the labours of my profession, the only questions I ask myself are, What is right? What is just? What is for the public good?
- Joseph Howe, Libel Defence, March 2nd 1835

The history of the Darby family is anything but a clear story. As with many maritime families, births, deaths, and marriages took place in various counties and countries, and sometimes on board of ships. Naming conventions saw parent's names recycled among their children, making it hard to tell who was who, and it was rare that women's stories were preserved at all. They were rarely discussed in business correspondence, which makes up a large percentage of the historical documents that have survived.

I stumbled across Joseph Darby's story one summer when I was hired by the Friends of Sable Island, a not-for-profit group dedicated to preserving the island and its history, to transcribe archive materials. The Nova Scotia Archives have a wonderfully comprehensive collection of original documents from Sable Island's early days of habitation, most of which are digitised, which made my job of transcribing that much easier.

In this collection, I found a jumbled series of log books and packets of letters written by a Captain Joseph Darby. Darby, I knew from reading books on Sable's history, was a bit of a ne'er-do-well; he was a disgraced superintendent who spent some time in the mid-1800s working at the establishment on Sable Island. Finding this a cohesive project, I set about transcribing everything related to Darby.

What I discovered was not a character sketch of a villain, but a story of a long and complex career spent saving lives and making difficult decisions. Looking at the whole picture that these documents presented, and especially the letters written around the end of his career, I saw that this bad reputation derived from the opinions of his employers. He worked for the Commissioners of Sable Island, who were wealthy political men from Halifax with a great deal more influence than Darby himself. They never set foot on Sable Island themselves, and as Darby's requests for increased aid and support grew louder over the years, they grew more frustrated with him. His dismissal from his post was partly to save face for the commissioners, and partly to brush off a series of unexplained and unfortunate circumstances on the island.

The purpose of sharing Darby's story is not to reposition him as a heroic figure or even as a "good" man. Instead, I have compiled select documents from his over forty years working on Sable Island to illustrate the complexity of the lives of the people who lived there, and the difficult position of the superintendent. With a fuller picture in view, we can appreciate that Darby's story is not so black and white, but filled with grey and up for interpretation. The challenges and situations he faced are ones that speak volumes about life and survival in the maritimes in the 1800s.

When it came down to assembling a picture of Darby's early life, I met my first challenge. Not only was his father also named Joseph Darby, but he was a captain, too. I managed to untangle the mislabeled web of letters by examining the dates and the handwriting. As you will see in chapter one, the father and son had different ways of signing their names, which made it somewhat easier to tell them apart. From the dated letters and receipts in the archive, I learned that Darby Sr. worked for the establishment on Sable Island from its inception, paving the way for his son's involvement.

Darby Sr. seems to have been born in South Carolina around 1759. He was a Loyalist, and fled to Florida around 1783, then on to Halifax, Nova Scotia in 1784. He settled in the town of Country Harbour in

INTRODUCTION

Guysborough County with his wife Martha Matthews, the widow of John Matthews, another Loyalist from Georgia. The couple had three children together: James Edward, Joseph Henry, and Martha Anne.

To provide context for Joseph Darby's story, I looked into the stories of his siblings as well. His older brother James Edward was born in 1783, and he married Rachel Elizabeth Campbell on the 7th of March 1807. They lived in Country Harbour too, and James listed his occupation as a carpenter on the census. It appears that he had a son. James and his brother Joseph were close, and worked together on ships and construction projects frequently early in their careers.

Martha Anne Darby was the youngest of the three Darby children and was born in 1790. She went by Anne to avoid the confusion of being named after her mother. In 1807 she married Archibald Cameron, a man at least 30 years her senior. The 1817 census lists them as living in Country Harbour too, with a boy and three girls.

The subject of this book and middle child of the Darby family, Joseph Henry, was born in 1787. The location is up for debate, but I found some sources suggesting he was born in the Channel Islands on a ship. When he was older, Darby married Mary Maria Stevens, a woman from London with family in Nova Scotia. His family base was also in Country Harbour, though he had a business in Halifax.

He and Mary had nine children together. Two of their names are preserved: Edward James, the oldest, who was named after Darby's brother and born sometime between 1810-1815. He followed in his father and grandfather's footsteps and sailed the supply ship between Sable Island and Halifax. His other known son was named John Henry, born around 1827, and he grew up on Sable Island working for his father during the superintendency years.

The three siblings, James Edward, Joseph Henry, and Martha Anne Darby, all died in the year 1863. The exact reason for this is unclear, but I believe that our Darby and his sister were living together in an apartment on Brunswick street in Halifax around that time. Through examining the burial logs for the Camp Hill cemetery, I located two small, unremarkable graves side-by-side where the Darby plots were supposed to be. One is marked J.D., the other A.D., which I believe is Joseph Darby and Anne

Darby (since that was the name she went by, and they were clearly made at the same time).

    I desperately wish there was some way to expand the story of this family with information about Anne, Mary Maria, and the other women named (and unnamed) here. Unfortunately, despite my best efforts, I can't produce any documents that speak about them with much detail beyond what you'll find in this book. The documents that were best preserved by the island's administrators were practical, and Darby wrote his daily log books knowing that they would be read by others — they were not personal, nor very emotional, beyond a strong feeling of frustration. The few snippets that mention the contributions of women on Sable Island speak to a much larger and important history that will likely remain in shadow.

    What we do have, however, is a story of a family's dedication to a cause that held significant weight around the Atlantic. The work done by the people of the Humane Establishment, and by Joseph Darby himself, meant that many families across North America, the Caribbean, Europe, Africa, and beyond were spared the tragic news that their loved ones, like so many before them, had wrecked and died on Sable Island. I hope the stories in this book paint a picture of this period that gives readers a new appreciation for this small but important piece of history.

Chapter One

Early Adventures of the Darby Family

Sable Island has been feared by sailors for hundreds of years. Called "The Graveyard of the Atlantic", its location 300 kilometres from Halifax off the coast of Nova Scotia puts it directly in the path of ships crossing the Atlantic from Europe to Nova Scotia or America. This critical trade route was littered with dangerous currents and deceptively shallow water near the edge of the continental shelf where Sable Island rests. Though the island itself is small, the sand bars stretch far beyond what is visible above sea level. Over 350 shipwrecks have occurred around the island since records started being kept.

Being the closest landmass to the island, it fell to Nova Scotia to invent a solution to this deadly obstacle of trade. Prior to 1801, the only inhabitants of the island were the seals, seabirds, and horses, with occasional salvagers searching for shipwrecks to plunder. But at the turn of the 19th century, the lieutenant governor of Nova Scotia, John Wentworth, ordered a Humane Establishment — a small settlement of hardy people with provisions and rescue boats — to be built on the island with a clear mission: to rescue as many people as possible from shipwrecks. Additionally, and perhaps to the greatest advantage of the province, it also served as a facility for preparing and shipping wrecked cargo and materials back to Halifax. The government made a profit off the unclaimed articles that the superintendent rescued and shipped to the auction houses in the Halifax shipyards.

To oversee this new establishment, Governor Wentworth appointed a superintendent and several commissioners, to whom the superintendent would report. The first commissioners were William Forsyth, Charles Mary Wentworth, William Cochran, Charles Morris, and Michael Wallace, though from preserved correspondences it appears that Wallace took on the bulk of the responsibility. These men were well known in Halifax and owned several large and successful businesses. Charles Morris, who shared a name with his father and grandfather, was the third in his family line to serve as surveyor general for Nova Scotia. The Morris family came to Halifax from Hopkinton, Massachusetts, and their influence extended to several industries.

Charles Morris' older brother, James Rainstorpe Morris, was appointed by Wentworth as the first superintendent of Sable Island. He was a retired member of the British Royal Navy and was in his early 50s when he went to the establishment. Superintendent Morris initially took three men with him as hired hands: Adam Moore, David Ross, and James McLaughlin. Edward Hodgson, who would replace Morris as superintendent in 1809, joined them soon after. As the establishment grew, the labour increased, and even more men arrived to help: William Frampton, John Hallet, John Gregory, John Myers, and Guy Morris (James' only son). Their families came with them, if they had wives or children.

The island was a thin spit of sand barely rising up from the ocean when James Morris and his men first arrived. With only remnants of shelters built by shipwreck survivors standing against the harsh winds, it was a desolate place populated by wild horses, seals, and seabirds. James wrote to his brother Charles five months after arriving on Sable Island to report the progress of the establishment.

Isle Sable, March 29th, 1802
   Sir,
   Please make known to the gentlemen Commissioners for the information of His Excellency Sir John Wentworth Bart. that all the people that were landed on this Island the 13th October last are at present in good health, and all the stock of cattle are alive that were landed, and in excellent order. The sheep have wintered independent of us, keeping a distance from us in general towards the NW bar in the valley. I often bring them to the stack of hay, which was very good but seldom eat any. They have lost three lambs, and there are four living, three more yet to lamb. The goat has lost her kid. The cows are in high order, gave milk through the winter. The bull we yoke and he draws well. The horse has been of infinite service to us. The hogs have no hair from the gristle of the nose to their eyes in front by rooting through the sand. I expect they will be a damage in the end. And the sows had thirteen pigs, but having expended all the corn in February, and the sows growing very thin, took off six and left seven, and now all in good order.
   I have been a long time anxious for an opportunity to acquaint you of our situation but none has offered since the twentieth of October. As from that time, there has been continual gales of wind alternately except a few days, and I am confident not five calm days in four months. Consequently was not able to fish or take the sounding round the Island. I never saw wild fowl so scarce in any part of America near the ocean as at this Island. We had killed only about 40, though often searched after them. Consequently our provisions are far expanded, there remains in store about 200 units pork, one barrel of bread, one barrel of Indian meal, one barrel of potatoes, which I intend to plant, about 20 units rice, 10 units peas, and 4 gallons molasses. We all must have suffered for bread had I not found flour and meal on the Island, as considerable of the bread and corn was damaged in landing and continual gales and rain from the third day after landing, which gave us many hard struggles once the buildings were in order, and having no bill of the scantling and several pieces lost creationed

another difficulty. But by making substitutes and by prayer and perseverance the store and house was put in good order under the smith of November, but surely the carpenter that framed the house was either in love or stupid, as many parts was wrong numbered, and no braces of any consequence to the building, which gave one a deal of trouble to affix the frame, as a building on this Island should be exceedingly well braced on all angles.

The 1st of February, I sent off a new constructed packet boat for Halifax, with a SE gale, and as is surprising to no one took it up as it was surely along some part of the East after missing thirteen days, with various winds returned. At this, sailed again within six miles from shore, she took her departure, and the papers all dry in good order. Should winds and weather permit the gentlemen that has charge of this, will come it to be safe delivered, and in the interim acquaint you of all the transactions on this Isle from the 18th of December to the present date, and is a man of an excellent disposition, William Burrows, Commander of the late unfortunate ship Maria *and* Eliza *of Boston, a fine new ship stranded on the South side of the Island the 16th December. Laden with salt from Rotterdam via Lisbon, bound for Boston, their lives were all saved, 13 in number, and most part of their provisions except bread which was mostly spoiled. The particulars of this catastrophe are entered in my journal, which I hope will be soon ordered before the gentlemen Commissioners in Halifax, that my Masters may observe in what manner the powers I am invigored with have been abused.*

The anchors, cables, some rigging, etc. are taken from the wreck and laid in a convenient place for shipping, the North side of the Isle about two miles East of our flag staff, where I shall soon as possible take over at that place the ship packet, two bower anchors, which we have nailed after several trials. I have also seized all the cotton that I have found on the Island. I expect 1800 units, which is at present in the possession of Mr. King. As simultaneous demonstrates to me that the most part of this cotton has been embezzled from the packet's cargo stranded last May on this Isle, which I hope will also be ordered away. And that family is, I am sorry to be obliged to say, they are dangerous people. I have been preserved on this Island from many threatening dangers, but in the main enjoy the blessings of health here. Companion had the misfortune to scald both her feet soon after moving into the house and suffered a deal of pain for six weeks. Otherwise, has her health well and in good spirits. Soon as possible I shall make a trial for fish, if unsuccessful shall try one of the wild horses, which I expect is good venison.

When I consider the situation of this Island, the distress of men and devastation of property, I am astonished in the meditation that no lighthouse has ever been erected on this Isle, for I am sure that if two lights was set on places which I have remarked, they would not only prevent vessels from running on the shore, but give aid to all that has an inclination to visit the Isle for refreshment, or to take a fresh departure, which in all probability would be of infinite service.

Thinking you'll be desirous to know my opinion early as possible, suggesting the lighthouses, how built and where best and most conspicuous, and as I have for a long time held the business in contemplation, I find it absolutely necessary that two be built, and in all the traverse of any mind, I find no method so easy, simple, so safe and so cheap as the enclosed plan for a lighthouse, my reasons and obligations as fully enclosed in my report book.

This Island has herbage sufficient to support 500 head of animals including bullocks, cows, sheep, goats, and rabbits. Only horses necessary for labour; all these wild horses should be transported in the manner of the Africans.

From your most obedient and humble servant at command,
James Morris
Charles Morris, Esq.
Halifax

James Morris created the first formal structures on the island, including a central station, two rescue boat stations, and several survivor shelters and lookouts. Later superintendents would improve on or rebuild these structures as they fell in and out of use over the years. The lighthouses that Morris suggested were only constructed after Confederation, over sixty years later.

Commissioner Michael Wallace was a pivotal figure in the early years of the Humane Establishment. Wallace was born in Scotland in 1744, and he and his brothers moved to the American South to set up a commercial trading business. This succeeded until he lost his property in the American Revolution, prompting him to relocate to Halifax around 1779. He settled on Hollis Street and resumed his trading business. It flourished thanks to the influx of other Loyalists, people who supported the rule of the British Crown, to the province; this included the Darby family.

Wallace received a series of appointments and titles, including the Sable Island commissioner role, by his friend Lieutenant Governor Wentworth. A Loyalist himself, Wentworth faced a great financial conundrum in sorting out all the Britain-supporting newcomers at the tail end of the Revolutionary War. He placed many of them in positions of power in the colony, and this, in turn, opened up further opportunities for other Loyalists.

This is how Darby Sr. became involved in Sable Island. Michael Wallace knew him from the shipping business, and he was perfect for the dangerous job of bringing supplies to and from Sable Island. Wallace held the Darby family in high esteem, and his sway with the commissioners was strong. Even thirty years later, just prior to his death, his influence saw the younger Joseph Darby hired as the new superintendent over Edward Hodgson's son, the anticipated heir to the position.

The earliest artifact that I found in the archives that related to a man by the name of Joseph Darby was a handwritten receipt given to Michael Wallace for some supplies purchased for the island. Joseph Henry Darby, the future superintendent, was only 15 years old at the time, meaning these early receipts and letters were written by his father. This is further confirmed by comparing their signatures. There is a noticeable difference in penmanship: Darby Sr.'s hand was brisk, whereas his son's signature was flowing and elegant.

This signature, from a receipt of hire in 1803, belongs to Joseph Darby Sr:

This signature, from a letter to the commissioners in 1832, belongs to Joseph Henry Darby:

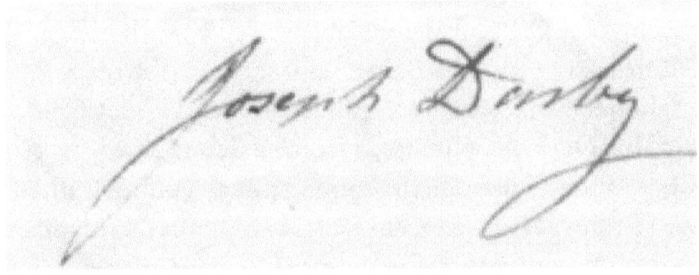

That first preserved receipt, issued to Michael Wallace on the 21st of April 1803, indicates that he paid Darby Sr. for some pork delivered to the island. Darby sourced this order, and many others, himself; the commissioners paid him out of the funds given to them by the government.

Darby Sr. was the owner and master of a ship called the *Eagle*. It was a schooner with a secondary boat, a shallop, of the same name. His receipts from 1803 reference both vessels. A shallop was a 17th century style of boat that varied greatly in style depending on where it was made. It often had two masts, square sails, and was used for transport or fishing. They could sometimes be broken down for transport on larger vessels. Looking into the Canadian Archives of Ship Registrations, there were two shallop-style boats called *Eagle* in Nova Scotia. The first one was registered in 1797, and built in Main-à-Dieu, Cape Breton. A note from a General Dawkins to the Sable Island officials in 1803 may hint at the fate of this small boat, which was noted to be lost:

> There may certify that I examined the bread and other perishable articles on board the Shallop Eagle intended for Mr James Morris of the Isle of Sable, a few days subsequent to her being bilged on the 15th instant at Fisherman's Harbour, that about one barrel and a half of bread was spoilt and that 14 or 15 bushels of potatoes was upward of twenty four hours under saltwater, The other articles of the cargo appear to be safe.
> May the 20th 1803, Gen. Dawkins
> To whom it may concern.

It seems to have been an unreliable vessel. The other *Eagle* shallop, registered in 1810, may have been a replacement. The main *Eagle* ship was the schooner, which is more difficult to date. It may have been an older ship that Darby Sr. purchased from someone else.

Wherever it came from, the commissioners routinely hired Darby Sr.'s *Eagle* to transport people, animals, and supplies. He crammed the hull of the ship with goods for the people living on the island, and returned with pieces of dismantled ships destined for the auction yards back in Halifax. His consistent employment says something significant about his abilities as a navigator. The shoals and sandbanks around Sable Island were notorious. Darby Sr. taught both his sons, James and Joseph, how to navigate these waters as they worked with him on board the *Eagle*.

During the years that Darby Sr. ran the supply route, his son Joseph Darby entered service on Sable Island as a member of the lifesaving crew. The following signed agreement bound Darby and another young man from his town to service for a year, and both ended up renewing their contracts after that period.

> We, John Myers and Joseph Darby, at present of Country Harbour in Nova Scotia Yeomen, do hereby voluntarily engage to go to the Isle of Sable as hired servants in the employ of government under the orders and direction of James Morris, Esq.,

the Superintendent of said Island, and we do each of us bind and oblige ourselves to obey all the lawful commands of the said Morris by night as well as by day, in boats or on the land, for the benefit and service of government, and for the protection of lives and property that may be cast ashore on the said Island, and we do further promise and engage to aid and support to the utmost of our power, against all disorder or mutinous conduct, of any persons that may come, or be upon the Island, and to resist and prevent any and every attempt of concealing or carrying away or destroying of property on the Island. And we engage to remain the complete space of twelve months from the day of our landing upon the said Island.

Our wages to be payable on a certificate from Mr Morris that we have in all things conducted ourselves according to the true initial and spirit of this agreement made at Country Harbour this day of July 1807. Signed in the presence of:

Edward Hodgson
Joseph Darby Senior
Joseph Darby
John Myers

Wages to commence the 25th August 1807, when they landed on the Island.

And with this document, another letter:

On behalf of the Government of Nova Scotia, I hereby agree to allow Joseph Darby and John Meyers three pounds currency per month each for one year from the time that they land upon Isle Sable, upon Mr. Morris' certificate of the faithful performance of their annexed agreement.

Michael Wallace
Acting Commissioner for the affairs of the Island
Halifax, 29 July, 1807

On the back of this letter is a note from a later date:

Joseph Darby left the service 30th May 1809 and paid off.

After spending two years labouring on Sable Island, seeing no one but his fellow labourers and the wild horses that roamed the sandy dunes, Joseph Darby returned to the mainland. This coincided with many changes on the island. In January 1808, orders came to Halifax from London that John Wentworth was being abruptly replaced by George Prévost as the lieutenant governor and lieutenant general of Nova Scotia. This same year, Thomas Jefferson placed an embargo against the Americans trading with Britain. Then, in 1809, Superintendent James Morris died at his post on Sable Island, leaving his assistant Edward Hodgson to take over the role. Hodgson was not keen to lose reliable young workers like Joseph Darby in this time of tumult, as he requested his return in an 1810 letter to the commissioners.

Isle Sable, 30th September, 1810
Sir,
I received yours dated 12th Sept 1810, and received all the articles all agreeable to your bill of sending, but I think, Sir, your supplies are very scanty. If there should be any wrecks this winter, I had not above two days supply of bread kind when the vessel arrived, and as for meat we have none, excepting horse flesh, that Mr. Darby can tell you, and the horn distemper prevail so bad among our cattle, so bad that we can't raise any to kill, for out of five calfs, we only raised one, and as for what the people say about they saving as much provision as supplied themselves, is no such thing, for they eat as much as four barrels bread belonging to the Island. But however I shall be more particular about it for the future, as I think beef a particular area of the expenditure of the provisions, and we tried to raise some oats, and had a very good appearance of a good crop but unfortunately a small bird we call the gray bird destroyed the whole. And the caterpillars were so numerous that they destroyed the greatest part of our garden. And as for the state of our stock, stands as follows:

9 cows
2 bulls
2 hair oxen
2 yearling heifers
2 spring calves
7 horses
25 hogs in all - very poor and nothing to feed them
John Myers is determined to quit the Island in the spring, and I wish you would look out for another to supply his place. If Joseph Darby Junior will come off, I would prefer him to any one else, he being a handy young man. Sir, you must excuse as the sea is a rising and time will not admit me to say any more at present and you must excuse me in cutting so short. I have a great deal more to say, but have not time to say it now,
    and remain your most obedient humble servant,
    Edward Hodgson
    P.S. I have enclosed Prince's account, and also a memorandum of articles wanting in the Spring.

Hodgson got his way the following spring and Darby returned to take John Myers' place for a time. In the following letter, Hodgson wrote to Commissioner Wallace with an update on the establishment's progress. He explains Darby was hired again to assist with the hay gathering season before the winter. Hodgson again emphasised the tremendous amount of help the establishment required in order to operate and survive the winter, and haymaking was no small task. The wild horses ate dry brush and the remains of wild peas that grew out of the meagre soil of the dunes, but the animals that lived in the barn would need ample feed to survive the weather to come. Not only were these animals important for their labour and byproducts, but they served as an emergency food ration for the people there, should the need ever arise.

Sable Island, July 28th, 1811
    Sir,
    I received yours by Capt. Darby and marked the certificate.

We have been at work every day that the weather would permit, ever since the Schooner Hercules *has left this Island, excepting one day that we went to the East End to catch the mare, as she ran away as soon was landed, and we caught her and brought her up to the West End, and she is a fine creature to work as ever I've seen. But Capt. Darby did not arrive here so soon as he expected for we had nothing but Southerly winds and thick weather for twenty days. And when he arrived, we had got eighty bales of cotton on shore and about 25 or thirty tons of logwood in and according to my rough calculations, we shall save about eighty bail of cotton for you and about 25 or 30 tons of logwood, and the two anchors, the windlass, the winch, the caboose, and the chain plates. And as for the deck nails that you expect are copper, are nothing but composition for we have tried several of them and we find nothing else. You mentioned about keeping a true account of the number of days that the men are working for you, which I shall be very correct about. I don't wish you to send any vessel till the middle of September, as I cannot attend to loading of it till then, as our hay making is coming on, and we must attend to that, and then we have got all the things to fetch across the pond up to the West End. Capt. Darby had to fetch his load over himself and his hands. Capt. Darby hired his son Joseph for you at Country Harbour at the rate of four pounds per month, which I am very glad he did, as he is a very good hand to mow, and about the hay, and the sooner we get done with it, the sooner we shall get to work at the wreck again. You must send some wood by the first vessel that comes, or else we shall have to quit the wreck to collect our winter's wood which is very scarce and at a great distance from the house. Capt. Darby says that his new Schooner will be ready to launch by the tenth of September, which will be a very good time and he says that he has plenty of wood, and he knows our situation better than any other man that comes here and I suppose he will come as cheap as any. I omitted mentioning in my memorandum for to send for some beans, barley, or rice to make soup, which I hope you will send with the rest of the things, and in doing this you will much*

oblige your most obedient humble servant,
  Edward Hodgson

More exciting events were unfolding in the world around Sable Island in 1811. King George III suffered from an illness and his son George became prince regent to rule in his stead. Tensions were growing between the Americans and Great Britain, and in May, the new Nova Scotian Lieutenant Governor George Prévost moved to Lower Canada — now known as the lower portion of modern Québec — to replace Governor Craig, and was appointed Commander-in-Chief of British Forces in North American. John Coape Sherbrook replaced him in Nova Scotia. Prévost was an experienced commander, having served during the French Revolutionary Wars and the Napoleonic Wars, and held this important post as the War of 1812 broke out in June of that year.

Despite its close proximity to the action, Sable Island appeared to have been little affected by the war based on the documents that survive. Their concerns were the same as always: receiving adequate supplies from Halifax, ensuring the safety of people and cargo from shipwrecks, and surviving the winter. Through all of this, the Hodgson family maintained their post on Sable Island, with the Darbys providing freight as always. This routine was preserved due to all warring nations recognising that the operation of the Humane Establishment was in everyone's best interest. *The Times* in London published a report in 1813, right in the middle of the war, about a meeting in Washington that included instructions given to the public and private armed vessels from the United States. It included this message:

> "The public and private armed vessels of the United States are not to interrupt any British unarmed vessels bound to Sable Island and laden with supplies for the humane establishment at that place. By command of the President of the United States, &c."

This refers directly to Darby Sr.'s supply ship, an unarmed British vessel, which continued its uninterrupted service throughout the war. Joseph Darby, however, was neither on Sable nor working on his father's ship during this time. In a letter written after his retirement to the then lieutenant governor of Nova Scotia, Sir John Gaspard LeMarchant, Darby recalled his activities during this time:

> "...in 1807, your petitioner, then a youth, was sent to the Island by his father to assist the Superintendent where he remained until 1811. That he subsequently piloted the Shannon Frigate, Captain Broke, and conducted her safe to Sable Island and brought away from thence the Captain, Officers, Crew, and prisoners of H.M. Ship Barbados, wrecked there with sixty three thousand dollars, and captured a most troublesome privateer called the Wily Reynard.
>
> That in 1814, your petitioner joined his father in the purchase of a smart Schooner named the Two Brothers for the service of Sable Island, of which he was the Master, and sailed under a protection or convention signed by the American Government and the Government of Nova Scotia against all public—"

Here the letter is cut short, as the second of three pages is missing. These brief lines reveal an exciting period in Darby's life, and an acknowledgement of the importance of the agreement between America and Nova Scotia regarding Sable Island's supply lines.

Darby was in his mid-twenties during the exciting chapter he mentioned in that letter. The HMS *Shannon* was a 38-gun *Leda*-class Frigate left Britain for Halifax as tensions escalated prior to the war. Joseph Darby was hired on as pilot for the ship by Captain Broke sometime between 1811 and 1812. As pilot, he would be responsible for navigation — a job that he was uniquely qualified for thanks to his experience with the dangerous waters surrounding Sable Island. The *Shannon* is memorialised for its historic defeat of the USS *Chesapeake* on June 1st, 1813. It is unlikely that Joseph Darby was still a pilot on the ship for this famous battle, as surely it would have merited mention in this letter detailing his life's accomplishments.

Darby does confirm that he was part of the rescue of the HMS

Barbados, which ran aground at Sable Island on the 29th of September, 1812. The *Shannon* was in Halifax at the time, and was sent to Sable Island with the HMS *Bream* to rescue the people stranded there. The *Barbados* had been en route for Halifax when it was caught by wind and currents and blown onto the shores of Sable Island, where it was quickly broken up by the fierce waves. Captain Thomas Huskisson and all but one of his crew of 195 people were rescued, along with a very expensive cargo — gold and silver coins, reported to be worth anywhere from $63,000 (as Darby states) to $500,000. The *Shannon* and *Bream* collected the people and cargo and set sail for Halifax. Along the way, the *Shannon* intercepted the American privateer schooner *Wily Reynard* from Boston.

The *Wily Reynard* was a notorious ship, owned by merchant Charles W. Green of Boston. First Lieutenant Thomas Swaine committed violent crimes with his crew, ignoring the fact that it was against international law for privateers to attack on land. One such incident was reported in Halifax newspapers: in August of 1812, Swaine and his crew landed on Sheep Island in New Brunswick, where an elderly man named Francis Clements and his family had a farm. Clements was murdered, his family was terrorised and assaulted, and his property was stolen as the *Wily Reynard* escaped. This incident in particular made it a high priority to capture the ship, as the story was highly publicised and of great concern to Lieutenant Governor Sherbrooke.

After the HMS *Shannon* encountered and subdued the *Wily Reynard*, they brought the ship and its crew back to Halifax. At this time the British government was sending captured privateers to a prison on Melville Island, and Thomas Swaine was first sent there before being shipped off to the infamous Dartmoor prison in England.

Darby's role as the pilot of the *Shannon* during these highly publicised events gave him a good reputation and credibility among the maritime community in Halifax. A little more than a year later, Darby and his father jointly purchased the Schooner *Two Brothers*, the name perhaps referring to Joseph Henry and his older brother James Edward. Darby became master of this ship, and for the next fifteen years, it was the source of his livelihood.

After Joseph Darby left Sable Island for his adventures on the

Shannon, his brother James was hired on by Superintendent Hodgson as a replacement. James appeared to make an equally positive impression as his younger brother did, adding to the family's already favourable reputation in this community.

> *Michael Wallace, Esq.*
> *Sir,*
> *I have received by Capt. O'Brien your letter and not having time to write by him, I have taken this opportunity by Capt. Darby and the weather not answering, I had no opportunity of putting any thing on board the Schooner* Munter *- there was nobody cast on shore this winter, but the next day after the* Munter *left the Island, there was an American Schooner cast on shore within two and a half miles of the house. Captain Naws and Schooner* Fortune *belonging to Chatham, Cape Cod, crews all saved and vessel high and dry, and the crew was taken off by Captain Atkins, Schooner* Nightingale *belonging to Cape Cod. I have detained the property on the Island until I hear from you. The Schooner* Fortune *was on a fishing voyage, there was about forty nags heads of salt, and the sails and rigging - I suppose it is not worth more than ten pounds. If there should be a vessel from the States, I have promised to let the property go off, detaining the salvage one third if this should happen before I hear from you. I have sent the oilskins and cranberries by Capt. Darby which he has signed a bill of leaven for, and as for the state of the land, I am very sorry to say that it is in a very low state; they have never been so low since ever the Island has been settled. There are three of the horn cattle dead, and two more of six put to die every hour. I am very sorry to tell you the mare is dead, she only about two hours sick. While she did live, she was in the greatest agony in the world. I suppose it had been the dry gripes. She had a very fine colt in her, and she was very fat herself.*
> *Capt. Darby arrived here the 19th. Very thick foggy weather and the winds from the Eastward. We have had a tolerable good time to load. I could not send you only three barrels of cranberries.*

I had the misfortune to lose a flat load coming down the lake flat and all blew entirely out of the water. I hope, sir, you will send the vessel back as quick as possible. By that time I shall have another load over for her. The logwood is buried as much as six feet under the sand, and take such a long time to dig it out, only for that I should have had it all over before now at the shipping place. James Edward Darby arrived here with his father and I think he will answer very well, as he is a smart, active young man. John Mines and Prince, the black man, have left the Island with their own desire. Now, sir, I have got three boys and they are pretty stout; one is 19 years and the other is 27, and the other is 12. I think, sir, these three are as good as two, and I hope, sir, you will take it into consideration and allow them something for their work. If not, I must send them off and set them into some kind of business. The anchors of the Combuse *I could not send, as the vessel was so much loaded, she was well slow, and I stowed her myself.*

I am, sir, with respect, your most humble servant,
Edward Hodgson

James Edward went on to establish himself as a carpenter, with his home remaining in Country Harbour instead of the more metropolitan Halifax, even when he worked on Sable Island under his brother's command later on. In the year 1818, Darby Sr. passed away around the age of 59. In the wake of this loss, Joseph Henry and the *Two Brothers* took over the supply route between Sable Island and Halifax that his father had sailed for nearly two decades. The contracts preserved indicate that it was business as usual as the Darby family continued to provide the most vital service to the people living on Sable Island.

Sable Island, May 25 1819
Received from Mr. Edward Hodgson, on board the Schooner Two Brothers, in good order and well conditioned, nine casks of seal oil, four casks of black fish oil, and four barrels of seal skins, which I promise to deliver to Michael Wallace, Halifax. Dangers of the seas expected. Witness my hand,

Joseph Darby

Not all of these contracts include a payment price, but occasionally the total is scribbled onto the slip.

Halifax, 9th June 1819
Received from Michael Wallace, Commissioner, for Sable Island, twenty five pounds for the hire of my Schooner the Two Brothers going to the Island with supplies and back to Halifax with oil and skins.
Joseph Darby

While £25 may not seem like a large sum for two perilous sea journeys in current value, adjusting for inflation over time shows that this would be the equivalent of nearly £2000 today, or around $3500 Canadian dollars. Darby counted on many of these contracts each year to earn his living, undoubtedly supplementing this regular business with other ventures and voyages.

The articles sent to Sable Island at this time were varied, but the regular provision shipments paint a picture of daily life. We can learn what food was being eaten, mark the activities and construction projects, and measure the growth of the establishment. One such list from 1818, including an exceptional number of items, reads as follows:

List of articles sent to Sable Island on board the Schooner Two Brothers, Joseph Darby Master, for the use of the Establishment there.

2 barrels mess pork
2 barrels mess beef
1 bag of barley
3 barrels of flour
2 barrels of Indian meal [note: cornmeal]
1 barrel of brown sugar
1 barrel of molasses
6 empty porter hogsheads [note: porter was a type of beer,

and a hogshead was around 250 litres]
2 porter hogsheads, filled with coal
6 bags of corn
6 felling axes and 1 broad axe
6 scythes
6 strong hoes
1 grindstone
8 lb salt petre [note: potassium nitrate, a food additive and preservative]
12 bunches onions
6 barrels salt
2 large kettles
1 planished saucepan
1 dozen pudding pans
1 1/2 dozen riveted pints
2 copper sprout lamps
3 bags lead shot
2 frying pans
2 plane irons
2 dozen panes window glass 7x9 inches
50 gun flints
6 barrels of bread
1 cask spirits containing 15 gallons
12 lb boat nails and 1 iron pot
1 boat and 5 oars
2 quintals of cod fish [note: a quintal was a unit of measure weighing about 100 lbs]

Received from Michael Wallace, Commissioner for the affairs of Sable Island, on board the Schooner Two Brothers, *whereof I am Master, all the articles enumerated in the foregoing abstract in good order, which I promise to deliver in like condition unto Mr. Edward Hodgson, Superintendent there, danger of the seas excepted.*

Halifax 20th August 1818
Joseph Darby

It was inevitable that Darby would pick up a great deal about the operations of the Humane Establishment on Sable Island from his many years of service in many different capacities. Like his father, he possessed an unparalleled familiarity with the treacherous waters that surround the island. This made him a valuable asset, not only to the superintendent and commissioners, but to the sailors and passengers of wrecked vessels who needed rescuing.

In 1822, Darby's expertise led to the rescue of the crew of the French ship *L'africaine*. On the 26th of May, *L'africaine* ran aground off the coast of Sable Island. Darby, about 34 years old at the time, had been Master of the *Two Brothers* for eight years and had an experienced crew. As he was approaching Sable Island with supplies, Darby spotted the ship stranded on the sand bars off the coast of the island. The waves were violent, and tore at the sides of the stranded ship, breaking it apart. Knowing the exact lay of the shoals, Darby ordered his cargo to be tossed overboard to lighten the load and raise the *Two Brothers* higher out of the water. He navigated the ship over to the stranded vessel, and they managed to rescue the hundreds of sailors stranded as *L'africaine* turned into a wreck. They were successfully brought to Halifax. The following month, the ship *Victory* brought the sailors back to France, and Darby received a medal for his service from the French government in October of that year. An article appeared in *The Times* newspaper in London about these events, printed on Monday, September 23rd, 1822. Though somewhat damaged, the preserved copy of the article is mostly intact and provides a translation of a story in the French newspaper *Le Moniteur Universel*.

SATISFYING ACKNOWLEDGEMENT OF BRITISH HUMANI-TARIANISM

The Moniteur of Friday last says — "the King's corvette [...] commanded by M. Behie, Capitaine de fregate, sailed from [...] on the 1st inst. for Halifax, on a special mission, the object of which was as follows: — "All the journals have announced the wreck of l'Africaine, *which, proceeding from off the Caribbee [...] to*

Newfoundland, encountered some thick fogs, and was wrecked on the Isle de Sable, about 80 leagues from the coast of Nova Scotia. The officers and crew of this ship owe their lives to the prompt aid and intrepid perseverance of certain subjects of his [...] Majesty. The Sieur Hodgson, head of an English family established on the Isle de Sable, his son-in-law, and one of their servants, formerly a seaman, contributed, at the peril of their lives to save eighty men, who made the first attempt to gain the [...]. The Sieur Darby, captain and owner of the English galliot Two Brothers, *whom a particular mission brought into that [...], who heard the signals of distress made by* l'Africaine, *without hesitation threw his cargo overboard, and entered the dangerous passages in order to render prompt assistance. After having [...] and narrowly escaped shipwreck, they succeeded in getting a portion of* l'Africaine's *crew on board, and during the passage from thence to Halifax, manifested the most kindly disposition administering to their comforts. Captain Darby's galliot not being able to take all the frigate's crew on board, Sir James Kempt, the Lieutenant General and Governor of Nova Scotia, sent his own scout to the Isle de Sable, which took on board the remainder. During their voyage to Halifax the officers and crew of* l'Africaine *received every consideration from this General officer and the officers of his staff, and were supplied with every thing necessary. They also acknowledge, in grateful terms, the good offices of M. Haden, his British Majesty's Consul-General, who zealously superintended the requisite arrangements for their return to Brest. The [...] on the report of these details, which M. de Clermont [...], Minister of the Marine and Colonies, had the gratification of receiving before him, has nominated Sir J. Kempt, Commander of the Royal Order of the Legion of Honour; and has caused his thanks to be addressed to M. Haden, John Bazalget, Brigade Major, Major Gore, first Aide de Camp to Sir James Kempt. Three gold medals, and one of them silver, have been struck to commemorate the intrepid conduct of the Sieur Darby, of the Sieur Hodgson, of his son-in-law, and of their servant. Pecuniary recompenses accompany these medals, and his Majesty has further ordained that these acknowledgements of satisfaction shall be conveyed to their destination on the ships of the royal navy.*

Delivering supplies and occasional acts of heroism aside, Darby's route also played a pivotal role for the island as a means of communication to the mainland. Without his service running letters and reports back and forth, much of the establishment's progress would have been hindered. The information he returned to Halifax was often as valuable as the cargo he carried; in 1829, *The Times* in London referenced this function:

HALIFAX
April 25. — Captain Darby returned from Sable Island on the 15th inst.; no wrecks during the winter; all hopes are therefore at an end as respects the safety of the Ariel packet.

The news was important, whether it was good and bad.

In the year 1823, Joseph Darby undertook something of a creative project. He illustrated and annotated a map of Sable Island, one that is still referenced today as a near-perfect historical snapshot of the shape of the sandy island. This document shows that Darby's expertise was as valuable as everyone believed. He marked out the shallow sand just below sea level, the sources of fresh water and buildings on the island, and numerous other landmarks and dangers. He included some background information in the margins of the map:

"To His Excellency Lieutenant General Sir James Kempt G.C.B., Lieutenant Governor of Nova Scotia etc., The Honourable The Members of His Majesty's Council, and the Gentlemen of the House of Assembly of this Province, by whose Bounty and Benevolence this Most Excellent Establishment is supported and preserved.

ESTABLISHMENT

This very humane Establishment was founded in 1803 by the Provincial Legislature, at the recommendation of His Excellency the late Sir John Wentworth Bar., then Lieutenant Governor, and has since proved the means of saving many lives. Every year vessels are lost. The years 1822 and 3 were particularly marked, as from L'Africaine, Hope *and* Marshal Wellington *429 persons were saved, who after escaping the dangers of the Surf, would otherwise have perished with hunger. A Superintendent and four men live on the Island, supplied with good boats and provisions. The Isle is visited twice a year by a vessel from Halifax.*

THREE HOUSES

One occupied by Superintendent on N. side, 9 miles from W. end. Another uninhabited also on N. side, 4 miles from W. extremity and 2 1/2 from W. end of the lake, E.S.E. 5 miles leads to Superintendent. Another uninhabited on S. side, 9 miles from E. end and close to E. extremity of the Lake. W.N.W. 9 miles leads to Superintendent. Three houses are not in sight from the Beach, but 3 or 400 yards from it and the same also from the Margin of the Lake. Those uninhabited contain provisions, tinder box, matches, etc. There are fresh water ponds as will be seen by chart, but wherever the surface is moist, fresh water may be obtained by digging from 1 to 3 feet."

Darby clearly outlined the accomplishments of the island, noting recent cases that he himself was involved with, like the *L'Africaine*. He is precise with his measurements and directions, and goes on to provide the reader with specific advice regarding dangerous areas.

"GENERAL REMARKS. Soundings decline regularly only on S. side but approaching the Isle from any other bearing whatever there is comparative deep water (10 fathoms and more) close to danger. Vide Chart. In foggy weather, vessels should not approach N. side or point of either Bar nearer than 25 fathoms.

Two Belts encircle the Isle, the outer a mile from the shore 2 1/2 fathoms. These belts are increased by gales and high winds raking the Island, drift the sand from them to the Bars. The Isle is composed of loose light sand and high Gales frequently alter its outline and appearance. The present description applies to 1823. The bearings are by compass.

When a vessel is on shore in a fog, it becomes of the utmost importance to ascertain her true position in order to save the ship or the crew. Lower a boat when prudent and observe the following:

If breakers extend:
N.W. and S.E., you are on N.W. Bar.
W.S.W. and E.N.E., you are on N.E. Bar.
ahead N. and then lie E. and W., you are on South side.
ahead S. and then lie E. and W., you are on North Side.

The prevailing winds are from E. to S. and from S. to W. when N. or Leeward side is comparatively smooth and therefore should be sought. See in the Chart a swash way on each Bar to save Lives get to Leeward by crossing either Bar (according to the Wind) at these places. No risk in moderate weather, but if the surf should appear too dangerous, land as you can or try to weather the Bar altogether. Having once got to N. of the Bar hard up S.E. or W.S.W. (as the case may be) for the Land, and take the boat ashore as near the House as may be convenient. The Semicircular form of N side is favourable for boats as under Windward curve a Lee is afforded from E. and W. winds, but with fresh N. wind this form is against a boat getting off the Land, therefore if ashore N. side push the boat right before the Sea for the Land, rather than risk getting to Leeward by crossing either Bar. If ashore S. edge of either Bar, Wind N. land on S. side. If ashore on N.E. Bar in tolerable weather, wind about W. you may land at the East end without crossing the Bar and (vice versa) if on N.W. Bar and owing to the inner belt high water is best landing. After landing, if owing to fog you cannot judge your situation, so as to shape your course to one of the houses, seek the Lake and then proceed.

N.B. Strong gales cause annual shifting of the sand on both bars, which in the course of years must alter their form and extent. I have given the form of the bars found in 1823. Mariners approaching the Isle are warned to keep the lead going and never go nearer on South side than 10 fathoms, or North side than 25 fathoms."

Prudent ships that wished to avoid collision with the island carried copies of this map on board. This was the case when Joseph Howe visited Sable Island in 1848 after Darby's retirement, crossing the ocean in the *Daring*, captained by Darby's eldest son. Howe includes the following in his report about his trip:

"The true position of the Island ought to be determined, and accurate information circulated through all the communities trading on the Atlantic.

On the Daring's *cabin table lies the Chart by which she is navigated, published in 18—. Beside it lies a plan of the Island, including bearings and soundings, published by the late Superintendent in 1824, and revised in 1829. Between these, discrepancies, frightful to contemplate, exist.*

Captain Darby, by whom my attention was called to this topic, and who has had many years' experience and great personal opportunities of comparison, believes his Father's Plan to be correct. If so, and if the Charts in general use by the Navy and Mercantile Marine, are as inaccurate as that which I found in the Daring, *the errors will appear by a glance at this comparative statement..."*

Even after twenty years, Darby's map of the island proved to be more correct than the navigation charts held by the British Navy.

Chapter Two

The Superintendent's Job

THE HODGSON FAMILY WERE THE primary caretakers of Sable Island for most of the time that Darby worked there as a labourer, and for all the years he ran the supply route. Edward Hodgson, his children, and his wife all worked in various capacities, with four of his sons on the payroll. In 1829, Hodgson's attorney Edward Wallace collected wages from the commissioners for the four sons, due for various years in the 1820s. John Hodgson worked for 50 shillings per month, William Hodgson worked for 45 shillings per month, and James and George Hodgson both worked for 20 shillings per month each.

In the year 1830, we see Edward Hodgson's son William signing documents and pay slips. It was their intention for William to take over from his father as superintendent of the island. This didn't go according to plan. For a short time, the commissioners took over the official paperwork, and then the signature of Joseph Darby began appearing at the bottom of all the preserved documents. Darby became the superintendent starting November 1st, 1830. William Hodgson continued working under Darby on the island despite these circumstances.

There were a few reasons why the commissioners might pick Darby for the job over William Hodgson. On the one hand, they were impressed with Darby and his many accomplishments, which were quite numerous and diverse by 1830. Commissioner Michael Wallace, as mentioned before, particularly advocated for him. More than anything, it may have been because the Humane Establishment was a government-run affair, and it would be questionable to have one family monopolise the island for decades.

The first recorded instance of Darby acting as the superintendent appears in a letter discussing insurance charges on a ship, the *Shelburne Packet*, which reads as follows:

> *Halifax, May 17th, 1832*
> *Gentlemen,*
> *On receiving the account current against the Schooner* Shelburne Packet *for the year ending November 1831, I find a charge of fifteen pounds for the premium of insurance on the vessel for one trip to Sable Island in the November 1830, which is a sum that I never expected to have to pay, as Mr. Edward Wallace told me he, (I believe) the direction of his father, the then Commissioner, that they would pay the insurance on that trip as it was undertaken at a late season of the year, for the purpose of sending me down to the Island, and for the vessel to return under another Master, for which risk the underwriters charged a premium of 10 percent. Hoping, Gentlemen, you will take this into consideration, and withdraw the charge from me as the whole of the service of the vessel will be lost to me by its being swallowed up in expenses, and Mr. E. Wallace will be able to testify to the fact.*
> *I remain, Gentlemen, your faithful and obedient servant,*
> *Joseph Darby*
> *To the Gentlemen Commissioners for the affairs of Sable Island (William Lawson, Edward Wallace, Edward Cunard)*

This testament to the difficulties of transitioning leadership reminds us that Michael Wallace, the long-standing commissioner, had both retired and passed away the same year that Darby became superintendent. His son, Edward Wallace, remained as a commissioner on the board, but didn't have the same biases towards the Darby family as his father.

Many changes started happening on Sable Island. Darby oversaw the construction of several new buildings: improved barns for the animals, refurbished shelters for shipwreck survivors, and outbuildings to store barrels of food and farming equipment. His love of seafaring saw new boats built, and old ones made more reliable. The most tangible of these changes for Darby, however, was his newly negotiated salary. A receipt for wages from Edward Hodgson a few years prior read as follows:

Halifax 26th July 1827
Received from the Commissioners for Sable Island, sixty pounds for one year's salary due to Edward Hodgson, Superintendent of the Island, to the 31st of December 1826.
Edward Wallace
Attorney to Edward Hodgson

His yearly salary of £60 did not vary over his many years as superintendent. However, Darby's first receipt showed a significant pay raise from what Hodgson had been receiving:

Received Halifax, 18 May 1832, from the Commissioner for the affairs of Sable Island. One hundred and thirty six pounds 13/4 for my services as Superintendent of that Establishment from 1st November 1830 to 31st December 1831.

£136.13.4
Joseph Darby

Darby was receiving more than double what Edward Hodgson had been receiving as a salary. Knowing that Darby was used to receiving upwards of £25 for voyages on the *Two Brothers* between Sable Island and Halifax, Hodgson's £60 salary would hardly be enticing. Given the content of Darby's later journals, he certainly earned his pay: the labours of the island were greater than any challenge he had encountered before.

In July 1832, Joseph Darby wrote a letter to Edward Duckett, the clerk to the commissioners, to discuss the state of the island. The hardships of providing food for the people and animals of the island echo the sentiments of James Morris upon spending his first season there.

> *Sable Island, July 20th, 1832*
>   *Sir,*
>   *I received your much esteemed favour of the 21st June, and with it the bunting, pepper, mustard, milk pans, bake oven, also a saddle and bridle, that I have bought here, the bill of which is enclosed. It is an article we want much, and I beg you will present the bill for approval. I also send you four young horses not exceeding three years old. Two of them have been rode on, and they have all been cut, and one well, the danger over with them.*
>   *Also three good mares, one of them I suppose the finest mare on the Island, none very old. I hope these will bring a good price, as I have another full cargo ready and would be glad to have the vessel back as soon as possible.*
>   *It is a very backward season here. I am afraid I will have some difficulty in procuring hay for our stock, which is increasing fast. Potatoes are just beginning to grow and look well some of them. Others have never come up but the seed rotted in the ground, although planted twice over, on account of the very cold weather.*
>   *Cabbage, carrots, and beets, we shall have none this year, but I hope to have a crop of turnips. Cranberries I think there will be none. Some of the sheep are dying. By showing those things to the Commissioners, you will much oblige.*
>   *Your very obedient humble servant,*
>   *Joseph Darby*
>   *To E Duckett, Clerk to the Commissioners for the affairs of Sable Island at Halifax*

Later in the month, when shipping horses to Halifax, Darby writes again to Duckett.

THE SUPERINTENDENT'S JOB

Sable Island, July 31st, 1832
  Sir,
  The vessel not sailing last night, I went on board this morning where I found one of the fine mares dead and Captain Thompson complained that he had no one to attend them, so that I have sent John Stevens off to take care of them, and has taken a very ordinary hand in his place, and to make the number of horses up I have sent a young horse in place of the mare that died. He has been cut about 10 or 20 days, and although not quite well, is perfectly out of danger, and will make a good horse.
  Yours sincerely,
  Joseph Darby

Darby would have been reluctant to send one of his reliable workers away, seeing as the island hands were critical to the success or failure of each year. John Stevens, his wife's brother, had been on the island for many years under Hodgson, and continued to be well regarded by Darby. Men that were familiar with the challenges of the island were valuable, as they knew what they were in for every time a storm rolled in. New labourers were unpredictable, as the isolation of Sable Island and the difficulty of the work did not agree with many people.

From his letters around this time, we also see that Darby had a friendly and almost patron-like relationship with the commissioners. A note from Darby to Edward Wallace testifies to this:

Sable Island, July 31st, 1832
  Sir,
  I thank you very kindly for the three smoked salmon you sent me, which was a great treat indeed, but I am afraid they must have been very dear and scarce this season.
  I remain yours sincerely,
  Joseph Darby

Beyond fulfilling the usual duties of the superintendent, Darby could provide insights from his seafaring experience, which provided new advantages for the establishment. It also meant fewer tasks and projects had to be outsourced. Darby was not shy about giving his opinion and was quick to volunteer his own services and connections where he saw fit.

> *Sable Island, September 11th 1832*
> *Sir,*
> *I received yours of the 8th of September with all the articles I sent for, in good order (except the pickled fish, which I would like to have part good herrings), also one barrel of pork, and one barrel of beef that you sent by her last trip.*
>
> *With regard for building a small vessel here, I have to beg you will, first, allow me to give you my own views, and secondly, to show you what I will actually want, and thirdly, what I may probably want.*
>
> *First, my idea as regards the vessel you now have, is a burden on the funds of the Establishment, by keeping nearly a double crew in her the whole time, and from the mariner in which they are and leaving the vessel every trip, there must be a great loss in the shape of advances. Under these circumstances I fear you cannot keep her and I don't like the idea of being left here without a dispatch boat of some kind. I think that a small vessel of about 20 tons, say 20 foot keel, 12 foot beams, 5 foot depth of hold, built flat bottomed with deep and broad knee boards, a very round side, with also a very round deck, with her floor heads and puttock timbers, seamed with plank outside and in, and bolted through firmly would be sufficiently strong to remain on shore any where on the North Beach. In the event of a gale springing up, and she should happen to be caught whilst the lake is open, there are frequent opportunities of getting in or out such a vessel, loaded or light, and at present the passage is very good, but yet not proper for my vessel to enter it. But one intending to stop here, as although the times of access and egress is frequent, get very uncertain, when in the lake once she would be very safe. Or in the event of not getting into the lake, and bad weather come on, she might be ram on shore on the*

THE SUPERINTENDENT'S JOB

North Side and hauled up. Two men from the Island could go to Halifax in her with dispatches, take our oil and skins, cranberries, and spring and fall, bring our necessary supplies by giving them something extra, for their extra service. A vessel's crew could take a fair opportunity and make the continent safely in such a craft, by having a gilet with them, and when there was much property on the Island, vessels could be freighted to take it away.

Secondly, for the building of such a boat, I would want a good working shipwright, such a man as John Walen, as I don't want information, but a man who is willing to work. I should want sails, rigging, cables and anchors. I should want nails for fastening the deck and ceiling. I should want about 40 small spruce knees, and about 50 puttock timbers, very crooked agreeable to a mould I would send you, I would fasten the outer skin with copper, and the other materials with the copper I think I could furnish here.

Thirdly, I might want, in the event of ever getting ashore on the beach, a good fall and blocks to haul her up, also I might want a good jack screw to shove her off.

Now the idea of willfully imposing on the Commissioners to bring them onto a measure that might be hazardous, or not productive of any good, makes me shudder. Consequently, as this is an enterprise that no one knows any thing about but myself, and that not from experience I was willing to try the thing myself, so that if it did not succeed, there would be none to complain, and if it did that, the property should be mine, that I should have the benefit of all the materials I would furnish here without any charge, that I should have the assistance of the hired servants here, that I should have some benefit from her afterwards to pay the expense of keeping her up, but if the Commissioners would rather build her themselves, I should be much better pleased, and when our other business did not interfere, I would lend any heart and hand to have her completed, and would send the moulds by the next opportunity for what timbers I should want, as I would wish to have her build here under my own eye.

I have shipped ten mares and horses and a colt, which I

hope will arrive safe. Our hay making this year has been so very troublesome on account of the weather that I had not time to make the necessary preparation for cutting horses. But I have done all that was in my power to do, and if you please to send the vessel again as soon as the weather will permit, I will endeavour to send you a few more horses, as there is a gale of wind coming on I hope that you will excuse haste at this time. Whilst I most humbly thank you for all your kindness and attention to me, hoping that God will strengthen your hands and bless your endeavours. I remain, with the truest respect and esteem, your most humble and obedient servant,
    Joseph Darby

    This letter reveals a great deal about Darby's character, and how he would approach the role of superintendent over the years. His enterprising nature, which the commissioners found such fault with towards the end of his career, is obvious — he was never content to work selflessly for the establishment without consideration for his own situation (and the large family he had to provide for). Aside from receiving a higher salary than his predecessors, Darby constantly considered his own business interests while performing the duties of the superintendent. This letter in particular would have placed Mr. Duckett in an awkward position, forcing him to represent Darby's clever phrasing to the commissioners, which would surely incline them to mitigate their risks by putting the expense of this proposed vessel on Darby.

    Darby sent another letter to the commissioners on November 12th of the same year. He was persistent when he felt he had a good idea, and didn't take well to being put off or ignored. This letter detailed the wreck and loss of the brig *Floyd*, and a few other details about affairs of the island. In a postscript, Darby not-so-subtly mentions how the boat he wished to construct could have made a difference in the rescue efforts, pointing out "here has been another opportunity for a small vessel to have been employed to advantage."

    The year 1832 ended without a sign of Darby's desired project, and a statement of the establishment provides a picture of the island at this time.

Statement of the Establishment with the wages due to the servants for the period ending 31st December 1832
    No. 1. Joseph Darby, Superintendent to the Establishment, one years salary to 31 December 1832. £100.
    No. 2. John Hodgson, a hired servant, one years wages to 31st December 1832 at 36 shillings per month. £30
    No. 3. Patrick McKeige, ditto, £30
    No. 4. John Esson, ditto, £30
    No. 5. John Stevens, ditto, £30
    No. 6. James Darby, ditto, £30
    No. 7. David Laurence, from 1 day March to 31st December at 50 shillings per month, £20
    No. 8. Benjamin Lunker, from 13 May to 31st December, 45 shillings per month, £16.17.6
    No. 9. Martin Shaffer, from 19 May to 31st December, 50 shillings per month, £18.6.8
    Total £305.4.2
    Halifax, 31 December 1832
    E. Duckett, Clerk to the Establishment.

With only one member of the Hodgson family left among the hired hands, and with both Darby's brother James and brother-in-law John Stevens employed, the shift in family power over Sable Island was clear.

The greatest resources available to provide insight into the daily activities on Sable Island are the superintendent's journals. These logbooks, which were periodically duplicated and sent to the commissioners for inspection, had an entry for each day of the year with pertinent details about labour division and island affairs. Each superintendent had his own style of keeping these journals, ranging from very spare and minimal entries to lengthy narratives. Darby's journal entries, while occasionally lengthy, were typically a few lines long with just enough detail to illustrate the day.

Unfortunately, the collection of preserved journals is incomplete. A card in the files at the Nova Scotia Archives provides some insight into this unfortunate circumstance:

> *25 September 1974. Mrs. P. Christie says that, according to Mr. Donald Johnson, Ketch Harbour, Superintendent of Sable Island from 1938 until after the Second World War, many of the record books and journals (some dating back to the early 1800's) were lost overboard in 1944, while being loaded at Sable Island.*

Despite this loss, several of Darby's journals still exist today. The earliest begins on the 1st of April 1833. Darby had been superintendent for about a year and a half.

Monday, April 1st
Commences with the wind NW and clear, fine weather. Two men are sawing, some hands hauling timber. This day ends with the wind NNW and cloudy weather with a light shift of snow.

Darby's journal entries follow this general formula, which was typical for logbooks in many vocations. Each entry begins with a survey of the weather and usually ends with the same. He notes the activities of the hired hands, details about the livestock and trade, and, when they occurred, the play-by-play of shipwrecks.

Tuesday, April 2nd
Commences with the wind North, and very light, with dark hazy weather. The people employed as yesterday. This day ends with the same kind of wind and weather.

Wednesday, April 3rd
Commences with the wind at North and fine moderate weather. The people variously employed. This day ends with the wind light and variable and fine weather.

THE SUPERINTENDENT'S JOB

Thursday, April 4th
Commences with the wind NE and fine weather. I sent one hand to the new house with a horse and cart to fetch up a pig, some hands making a fence, two hands a sawing. The man returns and reports J Hodgson picked up a sheep drowned on the North beach. This day ends with the wind SSE and looks like bad weather.

Friday, April 5th
Commences with the wind S by E, and rain and thick weather, and ends with the wind SW and thick fog.

Saturday, April 6th
Commences with the wind WSW and dark thick weather. I sent some hands round the store. A man went round the SW bar, and found a new pump belonging to some small vessel, the upper part painted white, also part of a new chair, bottom painted dark mahogany colour, with bright yellow rings around the legs. This day ends with the wind NW and dark cloudy weather. Some hands setting out turnips, carrots, beets, and cabbage stalks, some hands white washing inside the house.

Though the establishment was successful at rescuing many ships, there were inevitably occasions when wrecks went unnoticed by the small staff on the island, or took place on distant shoals that they could not reach safely. Haunting entries appear over the years, noting items that washed up with no sign of a ship or survivors. It was the job of the labourers and the superintendent to find these sad remnants, haul them up to a storage building, and catalogue them so they could be shipped back to Halifax. If they found food that was still edible, they ate it. If they found supplies they desperately needed, they used them. But most of the wrecked materials were parts of ships, and these could be reused by boatbuilders on the mainland and sold for a for a profit by the government.

Darby occasionally recorded interesting sights in his journal. On April 7th 1833, he spied a fish about 12 feet long in the distance, which he identified as a sunfish. He sent five men out in a boat the next day to find it, and after hauling it ashore, they took the fat off it for oil — about 20 gallons in all. They used this oil was used for everything from lighting lamps to greasing wheels to cooking, when needed.

Darby's two eldest sons worked on the island for their father from the start of his term as superintendent, but only merited their own salaries after a few years. They were Edward James and John Henry Darby, and in the year 1833, they would have both been around 15-18 years old. They assisted with various projects, but were most often sent to search the island for supplies or carry messages between the outposts. On April 9th of that year, Darby had them take a horse and cart to collect cranberries, but the boys returned a few days later with only a half bushel all smashed to pieces. This was all they could find, and there would be no fresh fruit beyond what they brought home.

As April progressed and the weather improved, the island employees focused on outdoors tasks. They painted boats in preparation for the summer and broke ground for vegetable gardens. On the morning of April 14th, the first person up discovered a schooner at anchor off the North Side. Darby took a boat and boarded as soon as the sea allowed, finding it to be the *Kiram*, with Captain Hawbolt for Halifax, on business to the island. They loaded materials from the wrecked shallop *Margarett* on board, including a sail, an anchor, standing rigging, running, sundry blocks, and 5 masthead irons. From the island, they shipped nine barrels of shims, and "J.H.'s wife and child went off in her for the benefit of her health".

J.H. in this entry refers to John Hodgson. Mentions of women in the superintendent's journals are rare and mostly consist of these sorts of incidents. There were no medical professionals on the island, and the wives of the labourers would occasionally take some number of their children to the mainland for extended periods of time to receive medical care. Whether anyone was actually unwell in all these cases is up for debate. This would have been a good excuse to temporarily flee the hardships of life on Sable Island for the comparative comforts of Halifax. Despite their exclusion in Darby's journals, all evidence points to the wives and daughters of the island employees having a large role in keeping the establishment running. The scale of the domestic labour required would have been overwhelming and required a large cohort of people attending to it, particularly in regards to cooking. There were finite ingredients to work with, and many mouths to feed — especially when a shipwrecked crew appeared.

On April 15th, Darby wrote the following entry: "Commences with the wind NW, strong breeze, and cold. All hands employed breaking up ground and hauling out manure. This day ends with the wind NW and moderate. My brother went home today, I gave him one pound of tea."

Darby specifies that his brother was on the island. This helps when trying to establish his family tree. James Edward Darby was his brother, while Edward James Darby was his son, named after the aforementioned brother. To add to the confusion, this son eventually started going by the name of James Darby as well, but this wasn't until he was older and working as the captain of the *Daring*, when his uncle had long returned to Country Harbour on the mainland to work as a carpenter.

The rest of April was windy and full of snow; Darby noticed it was unusually cold for the season. When May arrived, they sowed the old gardens with oats and turnip seeds, and planted a great number of potatoes. Potato planting took up a lot of time, as it was one of the few crops that had the potential to grow in abundance in the sandy soil of the island.

While Darby and his family lived at the main station near the centre of the island, there were smaller stations set up at either end which housed a man and his family in a sort of second-in-command position. Part of Darby's job was to ration out the supplies that were delivered by ship on an irregular schedule. This was a task he took quite seriously. Nothing in the storerooms went unaccounted for, and rations were divided according to the number of working and idle people at each station.

The folks stationed at the distant outposts came to the main station occasionally for new loads of provisions. The items were fairly regular, as they received staples from the mainland whenever the commissioners organised deliveries. On May 24th, Darby recorded what he gave John Hodgson. "I gave him 40 lbs sugar, 40 lbs rice, 90 lbs of biscuit, 17 lbs of oatmeal, 1 quart of vinegar, 10 lbs of coffee, 8 lbs of fine salt, 1 lb of tea,

1/2 gallon of rum, 1/2 lb of mustard, 1 lb of pepper, 1 lbs of powder, 3 lbs of salt, 1 peck of beans, 1 barrel of beef, 1/2 barrel of pork, 4 gallons molasses, 5 dozen of mackerel." He sent another man with a cart with Hodgson to get all these things back home safely.

Taking care of the domestic animals was an important job that everyone shared. Darby recorded the birth of a calf in late May, and a hunting trip where two small lake seals were killed. After a horse ran away, he sent men out looking for him, but they had no luck in tracking down the animal, which had likely hidden itself among the populations of wild horses. The animals were counted, managed, and rationed just as well as the employees on the island.

While Darby focused on the everyday affairs of island life, elsewhere in the world, people were concerning themselves with bigger ideas about Sable Island's management. On Monday, June 3rd, an opinion piece appeared in *The Times* in London:

> NORTH ATLANTIC OCEAN
>
> *Vessels bound to Halifax have the additional risk of stumbling upon that gigantic sand-bank, Sable Island: several vessels have thereon terminated their voyages. The establishment which has been formed there for the relief of ship-wrecked mariners is creditable to the humanity of the Colonial Assembly of Nova Scotia; but such can only mitigate, not prevent, the evil. That the mother country does not cause a lighthouse to be erected on some convenient point of the island is not only surprising, but greatly to be regretted. Why not make a second Ascension of it? Surely, in a circuit of 30 miles, some sort of productive soil might be found besides sand; at least, where the juniper, blueberry, vetch, and grass thrive, it might be possible to grow culinary vegetables, and to rear stock. It has fresh-water ponds, and sand-hills are elevated 140 feet above the level of the sea. The establishment of a lighthouse on Sable Island is well worthy of the consideration of our Colonial Government.*

Given the daily labour Darby recorded, we can only imagine the sort of affronted retort he might give to such a piece. While a lighthouse

THE SUPERINTENDENT'S JOB

might have appeared helpful and obvious to people unfamiliar with the particulars of Sable Island, the reality of the situation was not so simple. Some of the commissioners worried that a lighthouse would attract ships with a false promise of safe harbour, when it was meant to deter them from approaching. Darby knew that, more accurately, there was no point of elevation high enough on the island to construct any light that could be seen at a useful distance. These reasonings, coupled with a lack of funding for the project, meant that it would be decades before any lighthouses were built on the island (and then it was done with more advanced technology). While this newspaper report does demonstrate a knowledge of the general facts about the island, it says nothing regarding the labours of its inhabitants nor about the actual dangers faced there. It appears that while the public were aware of Sable Island, the specifics of the establishment were not largely known.

Around the 14th of June, Darby starts the men building a new vessel for use of the island. "I sent 4 hands with the teams to get a stick of timber for a heel for the vessel, and one hand to the new house to bring up J.E. Darby to work at the vessel," he wrote. The following day, the employees were busy hewing out the heel from the piece of wood they found.

As they made progress on the new boat, signs of a missed shipwreck began to appear on the shores. James Darby came up to the main station with a report of a boat washed up on the North East Bar. Inside were five seal gaffs, two pea jackets, and two packages of boiled pork. John Hodgson picked up two spruce oars with *J Herald* branded on them along the shore. A few days later, he returned with more evidence of a missed wreck. "John Hodgson came up today," Darby wrote on June 27th, "reports of finding a man's leather cap trimmed with white seal skin, and I now entertain fears that people have been lost in the boat which came on shore on the 15th instant." Even without a major storm having taken place, accidents at sea were too common.

Darby sent three hands around the island to bring up pieces of oak timber to saw for plank for the new vessel. Construction materials were scattered around the island, variously available depending on the amount of sand covering them. A man from the east end found a piece of timber too heavy for five horses to haul, so Darby sent him back with a yoke of oxen and another horse. This produced a piece of white oak 20 feet long and 21 inches deep, ideal for the construction project.

By the end of the month, Darby reported they were "getting on very fast with the vessel, having her now nearly all timbered in." This entry is the last preserved from Sable Island during the 1830s, the rest having been likely lost in the sea. The next journal by Darby picks up nearly ten years later, in 1842. However, other extant letters and documents shed light on these missing years.

While Darby's first proposal for a ship in 1832 seemed to go unanswered for some time, a formal agreement for him to oversee the construction of a ship for the island did appear in 1834. This is interesting, as from the journal entries above it appears that Darby had already begun construction on said ship the year prior to the agreement.

> *Be it remembered that on this eighth day of June in the year of our Lord one thousand eight hundred and thirty three, it is agreed by and between James H Tidmarsh of Halifax in the County of Halifax and Province of Nova Scotia Esquire, one of the Commissioners for the management of the Establishment on Sable Island, for and on behalf of himself and other the said Commissioners, and Joseph Darby, at present of Halifax in the County and Province aforesaid. Yeoman in manner and form follows to wit the said Joseph Darby for himself, his heirs, executors, and administrators for the considerations here aforementioned, doth hereby covenant with the said James H Tidmarsh, his heirs, executors, administrators and assigns that he, the said Joseph Darby, shall and will within the space of the year from the date hereof, in a good and workmanlike manner, according to the best of his art and skill at the Isle of Sable aforesaid, well and substantially erect and build, finish and thoroughly complete in every respect to the satisfaction of the said James H Tidmarsh and other the said Commissioners, one ship or vessel according to the draught or scheme hereunto annexed; the said vessel to have twenty eight feet keel, twelve feet beam, and five feet hold. The said Joseph Darby to find and provide at his own expense all and every description of*

materials which may be required in the building and completion of said vessel and in the fitting up and furnishing the cabin thereof, and also to furnish and provide one strong substantial hemp cable and one chain cable, two anchors, one compass, one boat, and the necessary and essential sails and rigging and tarpaulins of sound and good materials, fit and proper for said vessel. In consideration whereof the said James H Tidmarsh do hereby for himself and other the Commissioners of Sable Island, covenant with the said Joseph Darby, his heirs, executors and administrators, will and truly to pay unto the said Joseph Darby, his heirs, executors, and administrators the sum of one hundred and forty pounds of lawful money of Nova Scotia, when the said vessel shall be fully and completely finished, and the several articles and furniture herein before mentioned provided for said vessel, and it is also agreed between the parties aforesaid that he, the said Joseph Darby, shall and may without any cost or charge, have the free use of any materials belonging to said Establishment on said Island, and also the aid and assistance of the several persons workmen connected with the same resident therein, at such times and so often as the said Joseph Darby may require their services in the building and completion of said vessel, providing the same do not hinder or interfere with the usual duties necessary to be carried on and attended to on said Island. And for the true performance hereof, each party bindeth himself, his heirs, executors and administrators unto the other of them his heirs, executors and administrators in the sum of three hundred pounds of lawful money of Nova Scotia. In witness of whereof the parties to these presents have hereunto their hands and seals subserved and set the day and year first above written.

Signed sealed and delivered in the presence of,
J.J. Sawyer
Joseph Darby
James H. Tidmarsh
Halifax, May 30th, 1834

By starting the construction of this vessel before receiving official orders, Darby decided that he knew better than the commissioners in this regard. This may have been true, as they were not in touch with the daily affairs of the island, and Darby understood the genuine need for such a vessel. But by taking matters into his own hands even at this early stage of his career as superintendent, Darby demonstrated a sense of superiority to their decision-making that would create the rift between the two parties in the late 1840s.

In the year 1835, a brig called the *Lancaster* wrecked on Sable Island. By now, Darby and his team had several years of experience managing shipwrecks and saving crew, but every wreck was unique. The weather, the season, and the location of the ship were all variables that determined how dangerous the rescue would be. If the wreck happened at night, they needed lanterns on shore to try and guide the rescue efforts, but lashing wind and rain made it dangerous. The people landed on the island as a consequence of the rescue were another matter entirely, as the records show their unwilling guests ranged from traumatised and grateful to furious and violent.

This wreck was detailed in this letter from Sir Colin Campbell.

> *Government House*
> *Halifax, 11th June 1836*
> *Sir,*
> *I have the honour of informing you that the Commissioners for the management of the affairs of Sable Island have this moment communicated to me the loss of the Brig* Lancaster, *bound from Dublin to New York with passengers, on Sable Island on the 21st May. The vessel had on board a quantity of whisky and porter, and the Commissioners are apprehensive of difficulty occurring if the passengers, 65 in number, are not immediately removed, as they have already been rather riotous from seeking all the liquor, there being no civil house on the Island to restrain them. The Commissioners have expensed to me a hope that you might spare a vessel for the removal of the people to this place.*
> *Beg, therefore, entertain a wish that one of the vessels under your command may be spared for this service.*

THE SUPERINTENDENT'S JOB

I have the honor, etc.
C. Campbell

From his meticulous rationing of supplies, Darby and the commissioners were acutely aware that a large influx of people on the island could spell disaster for them all. With the supply ships coming from Halifax at unpredictable times, Darby never knew how long it would be until he could receive more supplies, or send stranded people on their way to the mainland. From his later journals, we see his acute stress any time the food stores ran low. This would be trying enough as it is, but the stranded folks sometimes were not very gracious guests.

The crew of the *Lancaster* lodged complaints against their treatment on the island after they returned to the mainland. As it was a government institution, complaints were taken seriously. The commissioners launched an investigation, which resulted in Darby needing to defend his actions and treatment of the stranded crew. Six depositions were produced, giving six different accounts of events, along with Joseph Darby's own testimony.

The charges appear to have stemmed from a man named George Cottingham, who had been on the *Lancaster* when it wrecked. He accused Darby of cruelty, of stealing materials from the cargo of the wreck, and of some sort of misuse of alcohol.

The first deposition came from James Norton, a labourer from Halifax:

> *James Norton of Halifax in the county of Halifax, labourer, makes the oath and saith that he was a passenger in the Brig* Lancaster, *John Miles Master, and was wrecked on Sable Island, and arrived in Halifax on board the Brigantine* Maria, *that whilst he was on the Island, and for about one fortnight before he left the Island, deponent resided in the house of Joseph Darby the Superintendent, and assisted as a labourer in saving the cargo of the* Lancaster. *That he was treated kindly by Mr. Darby as were all passengers, that George Cottingham resided also in Mr. Darby's house, and a few days previous to deponent's departure*

from the Island, several articles were missed and suspicion fell on the said George Cottingham, who denied the theft at first, but afterwards the articles having been found in his possession, he confessed his guilt and was dismissed from the house. That since deponent's arrival, he has heard the Lord Cottingham say that he would make Darby suffer for his treatment of him whilst on the Island. That during the voyage and since his arrival in Halifax, the Lord Cottingham associated chiefly with the sailors of the Lancaster *and not with the passengers. That deponent never perceived any secrecy on the part of Mr. Darby, nor concealment of any goods about his Establishment. Deponent was permitted to go into any room in the house, and has frequently been through the outhouses and never saw any merchandise deported there and does not believe that any could have been concealed from him with the privilege he possessed of access to all the sheds and outhouses. That deponent assisted in landing the cargo from the Lancaster, that the Captain set the Brig on fire to enable them to remove the cargo and one or more of the casks of whisky were burned. Deponent saw one with a hole the size of his hat in it, and was informed that the liquor it contained was spoiled, having been mixed with salt water. Thus deponent assisted in removing the sails saved from the* Lancaster *and shipping them on board of the* Maria, *and all the sails which were saved, deponent verily believes were sent to Halifax. Deponent further saith that Mr. Darby's whole conduct towards the passengers was humane and benevolent, and guiltless him to their approbation and gratitude. Deponent further saith that about five or six days ago, one of the sailors by the name of William Hill asked deponent for a hand kerchief which he had received at Sable Island so that he may exhibit it against Mr. Darby. That deponent refused, alleging that the only handkerchief he had retained there was given to him with some biscuits hid in it by the son of Mr. Darby for sea stores, and was old and of little value, that the reason biscuits was given deponent was because having lived in Mr. Darby's house, no regular ration had been weighed to him as to the other passengers.*

THE SUPERINTENDENT'S JOB

Swore to before me this 12th July, 1836
James Naughton

According to Naugton, Cottingham was the one at fault rather than Darby. This testimonial lines up with what the other witnesses had to say. The second deposition came from Edward Daley, a hosier from Halifax:

Edward Daley of Halifax in the county of Halifax, hosier, maketh oath and saith that he was a passenger on board the Brig Lancaster *when wrecked on Sable Island, and arrived here in the Brig* Maria, *that during the time he remained on the Island he lived in the house of Joseph Darby, the Superintendent, who treated him with kindness and benevolence. That deponent never saw any porter or whiskey used by Mr. Darby as stated and alleged in the affidavit of George Cottingham; whilst the Captain of the* Lancaster, *John Miles, resided with the said Darby, porter was occasionally drank by him, and deponents saw a bottle of whiskey on table, but after the departure of the said John Miles, deponents here never saw either porter or whiskey used by the said Darby, except on one occasion when he took a bottle out of a barrel which was left by the said John Miles in the store with three or four bottles in it, and gave a glass to this deponent and drank a glass himself. That deponent never saw silks or cloth as sworn by the said George Cottingham about the Establishment on the Island, and as Mr. Darby reposed confidence in deponent, he had access to all the outhouses of the Establishment and must have seen them. That deponent saw the blue cloth and waistcoat patterns given by Mr. Darby to George Cottingham, there was about one yard and a quarter of the cloth. It had been wet with salt water, was damaged and rotten, and he told deponent it was not fit to make up into a jacket; that the patterns contained three quarters of a yard rack or thereabouts, and one of them in the possession of deponent, they were damaged, stained and scarcely worth any thing. That deponent was in the sheds at Darby's at different times, one contained potatoes and another was used as a place of confinement for several of the crew who were refractory and had misbehaved themselves, and deponent does not recollect having seen more than two sheds, and is confident, if goods have been secreted there, he must have seen them. That no concealment was resorted to by Mr. Darby or his family, deponent was allowed to go into any part of the house and Establishment and must have seen bulky articles such as Cottingham states were deported there. That frequently remnants of cloth and merchandise are thrown up on the beach, but so wet with salt water that they were worthless, and deponent having picked up several pieces of that kind of stuff, Mr. Darby asked deponent if they were of any value or worth saving as he would take care of them and send them to Halifax. That deponent knows that some whisky was mixed with salt water and destroyed, he never tasted it, but heard the crew and passengers talk of it, and it was generally believed and notorious. That deponent knows George Cottingham, who did not reside at Mr. Darby's at first, but after three or four days he asked deponent to interest himself to obtain permission for him to reside there; that he, the said Cunningham, slept in a room with one of Mr. Darby's children, and stole several articles of clothing from some of the men belonging to the Establishment. That this deponent was present when Cottingham opened his box or trunk, received the articles from him, and returned them to Mrs. Darby, that Cottingham confessed that he had committed the theft, and was dismissed by the said Darby from his house and not allowed to return. That on the passage from the Island, Cottingham asked deponent whether he thought Mr. Darby had sent information of the theft, and said he was apprehensive that he would be imprisoned on his arrival at Halifax. That deponent had frequent opportunities of remarking Mr. Darby's good conduct and scrupulous attention to saving property, and remembered a box directed to Dr. Power of New York being saved from the* Lancaster, *and seeing that it was wet, he called on the deponent to be present when he opened it to dry the contents and take an inventory thereof, which deponent did. That deponent saw the sailors making trousers out of some of the sail cloth, and knows that they had got possession of some whiskey and were frequently intoxicated, and on one occasion saw Mr. Darby taking a bottle from them and breaking it to pieces. That deponent was allowed to remain in the cabin of the* Maria *on her passage and can not depose as to the conduct of the passengers in the hold. Deponent saw the cargo stowed, the whisky was below, and the sails on top to prevent access to the former, and deponent does not believe that any change or embezzlement of the sails took place. That deponent knows Robert Reside who was treated very kindly by Mr. Darby, but since his arrival in Halifax has used threatening language in the hearing of deponent, saying that he would make the bugger on the Island, meaning Darby, suffer for the non payment of his (Reside's) wages and expressions of that nature. And this deponent further saith that the whole conduct of Joseph Darby was upright, honest, and humane, and that the charges against him deponent verily believes are unfounded.*

Swore to before me this seventh day of July 1836
Edward Daley

The third deposition came from Samuel Lewis, a master mariner:

Samuel Lewis of Halifax in the County of Halifax, mariner, Master of the Brigantine Maria, *being duly sworn, deporteth and saith that he was employed by the Commissioners to repair to Sable Island to remove the cargo and passengers saved from the Brig* Lancaster *wrecked on said Island, that he was detained there four days, that he dined one day with Mr. Darby the Superintendent and saw no porter on table, that he was constantly occupied loading the* Maria, *but whenever he had an opportunity of seeing Mr. Darby, he was actively employed in removing the materials from the* Lancaster, *and was perfectly fatigued and worn down by his continual exertions. That deponent previous to leaving the Island was requested by the said Joseph Darby to examine two casks of whisky to ascertain whether they were in a fit state to be removed. That deponent accompanied the said Darby, tasted the whisky, and found that it was mixed with salt water and perfectly nauseous to the taste and useless, and deponent advised the said Darby not to ship it as the casks were barrels and leaky, and it would be necessary to put it in other packages and delay this deponent longer than was prudent, and when it should reach Halifax it would be thrown away as valueless. That deponent knows George Cottingham, a man employed to make some clothes or repair them for the said Joseph Darby, and he was detected in dishonest acts by Mr. Darby and thrown out of his house. That deponent had an opportunity of visiting any of the stores on Sable Island, there was no disguise used by Mr. Darby and if cloths, silks, and cottons were on the Island in the quantities sworn to by the said Cottingham, deponent thinks he must have seen them. That the passengers were extremely insubordinate and disorderly, and behaved so riotously that the said Darby was compelled to put hand cuffs on two of the ringleaders and confine them, and after they were embarked on board the* Maria, *they broke open the porter casks and embezzled part thereof. That deponent brought all the sails from the Island which were delivered to him by Mr. Darby and the same were placed in custody of the Commissioners aforesaid and sold, that they were not changed to deponent's knowledge, and deponent missing a topmast studding sail belonging to his own ship thinks that it was sold in addition to those saved from the* Lancaster. *That deponent does not believe the charges made against Mr. Darby, who appeared vigilant to protect the interests of the owners of the* Lancaster *and cargo, and examined the trunks of the passengers before they were put on board the* Maria, *a precaution deponent thinks a guilty man would not venture to adopt. That deponent was requested by Mr. Darby to let two families named Daley and Brady have accommodations in the cabin, which he did in consequence of reputability. Deponent further saith that if by possibility any sail was changed, it must have been with some sail belonging to the* Maria, *all of which were equally good if not better.*

THE SUPERINTENDENT'S JOB

Sworn to before me this seventh day of July, 1836
Samuel Lewis

The fourth deposition came from Alexander Barron, a mariner:

Alexander Barron of Halifax in the county of Halifax, mariner, late of the Brigantine Maria, *maketh oath and saith that he was in the* Maria *and Sable Island, and assisted as mate in managing said vessel and taking in the cargo. That eighteen sails were received on board the* Maria, *and delivered at Halifax. They were represented to have been saved from the* Lancaster, *that the whisky was stowed in the hold and the sails on top of it to prevent the passengers from getting access to it, that after the cargo was landed at Halifax, one of the sailors of the* Maria *told deponent that two of the sails had been removed from the hold and were in the forecastle. Deponent immediately caused the same to be removed to the place of sale. That some of the passengers broke open several casks of porter and used the contents. That deponent knows George Cottingham and he informed deponent that Mr. Darby had turned him out of his house. That deponent enquired the cause from the other passengers and was informed that he had been guilty of or suspected of theft. That the weather was tempestuous and deponent did not leave the Maria during the voyage.*
Sworn to before me this sixth day of July, 1836
Alex Barron

The fifth deposition was from Thomas Brewer, a yeoman:

Thomas Brewer of Halifax in the county of Halifax, yeoman, maketh oath and saith that he was employed to take charge of provisions sent in the Brigantine Maria *to Sable Island for the crew and passengers of the* Lancaster, *and to serve them out to them until their arrival at Halifax. That deponent lived in the house of Joseph Darby, the Superintendent of the said Island,*

and dined at the same table every day. That Darby here used porter to deponent's knowledge, that he exposed himself pleased at deponent's arrival, said the passengers and crew of the Lancaster had behaved infamously and conducted deponent round the Island to see the mischief they had done. That deponent was informed and believes that the night before his arrival, they had broken into one of the stores, that whisky had been drawn from the casks into bottles, a great number of which deponent and the said Darby found buried in the sand, and also bottles of porter. That most of the passengers and crew were continually intoxicated and extremely insubordinate and riotous, that the first mate of the Lancaster *and another man called Baker attempted to break into Mr. Darby's house, and the former threatened to shoot Darby, in consequence of which it was necessary to put him in irons, and send them by force on board the* Maria. *That deponent was requested by Mr. Darby to taste two casks of whisky which were leaky, one of which was about half full and the other three fourths full, that it was mixed with salt water and was of no use or value, deponent advised him not to ship it to Halifax. That deponent went through almost all the buildings on that part of the Island where Darby resides, and verily believes he was in all the outhouses attached to the Establishment, and never saw any silks, cottons, or cloths as sworn to by George Cottingham, and deponent thinks a knowledge of them could not have been concealed because he accompanied Darby and heard the abuse of the people when dissatisfied or intoxicated, but never heard dishonesty imputed to him. That deponent was informed by Mr. Darby that he had detected George Cottingham in theft, and turned him out of his house. That deponent never saw caskets of porter in or about Darby's house, nor any porter used by him unless he might have drank a few bottles picked up as above stated, but deponent implicitly believes that great depredation was committed by the crew as they were constantly drunk. That deponent saw them destroying rabbit warrens and remonstrated with them, and Darby gave additional provision to prevent the destruction but to no purpose. That deponent removed the sails of the* Lancaster *from the store to the* Maria *and took a list of them, and the same sails were delivered at Halifax. That deponent has heard the affidavits of George Cottingham and Robert Reside and does not believe the charges and allegations therein against Mr. Darby as deponent found him active, vigilant, and right in the conduct, and saw him examine the trunks of every passenger before they were sent on board the* Maria, *and in some, articles were found belonging to the Island. That deponent has heard the said Robert Reside say that he would ruin Darby if he did not obtain payments of his wages, and since his arrival in Halifax, he said Reside told deponent that he intended to swear that Darby had stolen a box of the value of one hundred pounds for the purpose of ruining him. That the threats of some of the crew and passengers were feared by Darby so much that it was necessary to keep a constant watch of eight or ten men every night as they had robbed the store and said they would set fire to it.*

Sworn to before me seventh day of July, 1836
T Brewer

The sixth deposition came from John W. Michael, a carpenter:

John William Michael of Halifax in the county of Halifax, carpenter, maketh oath and saith that he was a passenger on board the Lancaster, *and worked on Sable Island and came to Halifax in the Sable Island packet. That he received every attention from Mr. Darby, the Superintendent, who exerted himself to save the cargo and materials from the* Lancaster *and was vigilant in protecting the property and interests of all concerned, that it was necessary to establish a watch over the property saved, and Mr. Darby took his turn as well as the people under his command. That deponent has heard the affidavits of Robert Reside and George Cottingham and cannot believe the allegations therein contained against Mr. Darby, as his conduct was directly opposite to dishonesty, and he was so careful that previous to the baggage of the passengers being shipped on board the Schooner, he examined the trunks, and deponent does not think he would have done so if he was conscious of having been guilty of embezzlement. That deponent was in about the house of the said Mr. Darby and never saw any silks, cloths, or cottons as sworn to by the said George Cottingham, and he thinks he must have done so if the goods were in an open shed. That deponent heard from the passengers who came in the* Maria *that after the departure of deponent, the said Cottingham had been detected in theft, and turned out of Mr. Darby's house. That deponent can not avoid giving his evidence in favour of Mr. Darby, who did all in his power to make the situation of the passengers comfortable and to alleviate their sufferings.*

Sworn to before me this 7th July 1836
John W Michael

These depositions were consistent enough to give the commissioners confidence of Darby's sympathetic character. Darby provided his own letter, too, written the month before these depositions were ordered. This was prior to his becoming aware of the charges made against him by Cottingham and Reside. This fact was taken as an adequate testament to his conduct.

Sable Island, June 21st, 1836
Gentlemen,
I received your much esteemed favour of the 13th of June last by the Brig Maria, *Captain Lewis, and am happy to inform you that the* Michael Wallace *arrived here the day before, notwithstanding contrary winds, and we have been as fortunate as to get her in the lake just as the Brig arrived, and the weather since not proving very favourable, we have not got on so fast in consequence. However, the things are all shipped as the Bill of Landing enclosed with the exception of two puncheons of whisky that are stove so bad that they cannot be shipped. They are each about half full, they have been burnt, and I find on trying the liquor that there is so much salt water got into it, as to render it*

THE SUPERINTENDENT'S JOB

useless.

We have had to keep a constant watch day and night and have had to hire one man for that purpose to assist us, but notwithstanding the watch, the store was broke open on the night of the 17*th* of June in the side. On the 18*th* I observed the sailors drunk and took a bottle of whisky away from one of them, and commenced to search for more, perceived another bottle which I destroyed. In looking for whisky, we found the mate in his hammock drunk, and the men that I sent to search his hammock for whisky, he got up and struck one of them, the rest pitched him out of doors. When he again attempted to strike, cursing and abusing us, and threatened at a great rate, I ordered him to be put in irons to preserve the public peace. He is one of those that was heard to threaten to break open the provision store if any one would pin him. The other fellow that was drunk, I shut him up in a cellar, which he broke the door of, and threatened and abused the men that put him in. I then ordered him to be put in irons, and locked up separate from the mate, and we had to keep watch all night with loaded guns. The next morning, I sent them on board the Brig, and at the request of the Master, I sent on board a pair of handcuffs for to put on the mate, should he deem it necessary. In the afternoon, I sent off two other seamen and one passenger that had been stealing out of the house, of which Mr. Brewer can inform you.

Enclosed also is a list of the persons victualled from the Island, taken from the mess book from the date of the logs of the Lancaster to the present date inclusive, which I have got them to sign with marks and explanations on it. Some of the passengers showed symptoms of scurvy, and to such I have given two pounds of flour per day in place of meat, with vegetables, molasses, tea, oatmeal, and medicines, and I am sorry to say that they have not only killed every rabbit they could find above ground, but have dug up their burrows and destroyed both old and young, notwithstanding I particularly requested Garnick the mate not to destroy their nests. I had the next day to go after him with four men and drive him and his gang away from their nests, and take away a dog from them and lock him up.

There is a box directed to Dr. Power, New York which I opened here and found it to be clothing in a wet state. I dried them and packed them up again after taking an inventory of them in presence of Mr. Daley, a copy of which I enclose you.

Gentlemen, if I may presume to give you an opinion as regards the carrying of passengers with wrecked goods from this Island to Halifax, it would be simply this, that if possible the goods and the people should not go in the same vessel, particularly liquor and in the present case, two vessels of 50 tons each or there about would have carried all the present concern. One might have taken the property and the other the people, and no risk, no anxiety, and no mighty preparations to guard against mischief. Light vessels are always better here than heavy ones. They can work to more advantage, and I have no doubt they can be had as low and rather lower. At the request of Captain Miles, I put one new cooking stove out into an outhouse for the use of the sailors, and he promised me that if they damaged it, he would make it good. They have done so with dancing and fighting. They have broke off the lower doors, and the stove is not worth so much as it was by forty shillings, for which I hope you will make a charge.

I remain, gentlemen, your faithful and obedient servant.
Joseph Darby
To the Commissioners for the affairs of Sable Island.

Following these reports, the commissioners made a report regarding the charges against Darby.

Report of the Commissioners of Sable Island on the charges made against the Superintendent of that Establishment

The Commissioners of the Isle of Sable report, for the information of His Excellency the Lieutenant Governor, that on receipt of His Excellency's comments through Secretary Mr. James, in relation to a complaint against Joseph Darby, resident

Superintendent of Sable Island, they instituted an actual investigation, and although they have been unable to inform Mr. Darby of the charges alleged against him, they think that sufficient testimony has been produced to remove the aspersions cast on his character, and they have no doubt when informed on the attempt to injure him, Mr. Darby will furnish further proof to establish his innocence. The Commissioners have in their possession five depositions of persons of respectability, and have received from Mr. Darby a letter by which it fully appears that no concealment was made of the whisky left on the Island, but that the same was destroyed, having been mixed with sea water. And still remains for orders from the Commissioners, that George Cottingham (whose deposition was submitted to the Commissioners) is a person of bad character, and after having received kind and benevolent treatment, had attempted to injure the individual from whom he experienced it, because detection in theft caused a withdrawal of confidence. It also appears that Robert Reside, the cook, has used threats towards Mr. Darby, and in the opinion of the Commissioners, is actuated by malevolent feelings towards him. The Commissioners will avail themselves of the earliest opportunity of calling on Mr. Darby for further explanation and proof, as they are anxious to ascertain the truth, and still retain the respect for Mr. Darby's character and confidence in his ability, which has hitherto subsisted.

As soon as the answer of Mr. Darby to these charges is received by the Commissioners, they will immediately transmit the same together with the affidavits above alluded to, for His Excellency's information and further orders.

Halifax, 8th July 1836
E Wallace
E Cunard
W Lawson Junior
Commissioners

The following month, word came from the lieutenant governor's office that he decided no further investigation was necessary into the matter, and that no case was made against Mr. Darby. Things returned to normal on Sable Island.

Chapter Three

Island Management

After ten years as the superintendent of Sable Island, and with an intimate knowledge of the dangers that the staff of the island placed themselves in, Darby had good news for his employees. The Board of Commissioners had decided that they should receive some compensation for property that they rescued to be sold at auction in Halifax.

Copy of proceedings of meeting of Commissioners of Sable Island on 6th April 1841

Resolved that a percentage on the net proceeds at Halifax on all property saved of one and a half percent annually commencing the first of January last be allowed to Superintendent, and the sum of one pound to each of the men for their exertions in saving crews, passengers, and property from vessels stranded on the island. Said compensation to be for each and every wrecked vessel, and to be allowed only on the production of a certificate from the Superintendent stating that the individual claiming such compensation had acted on the occasion with all diligence, actively, and properly in saving both lives and property, otherwise the same shall not be awarded to him.

> *E. Wallace*
> *E. Cunard*
> *Wm. Lawson Jr.*
> *Commissioners, Sable Island*

This would not only supplement their small salaries, but would provide a great incentive to take more care and diligence in rescuing stranded cargo and lost articles on the shores of the island. The subtext of this new bonus was that the commissioners were growing suspicious about how things were managed on the island. They had no real way of knowing whether all the wrecked property was being declared, or whether anyone — Darby, specifically — was skimming off the top. Since none of the commissioners wanted to visit Sable Island personally, they only had second hand reports to rely upon, and they received the complaints from any unhappy people that had wrecked on the island. They assumed that a monetary reward for honesty would outweigh any incentive to profit from undeclared property.

They were right in assuming the workers on Sable Island were motivated by money — that was the main reason they agreed to live there, after all. But the enterprising Darby did not rest at this bonus. In 1842, he sent an impressive letter to the commissioners arguing for a higher salary. He makes a strong case for himself, and provides us with an overview of his accomplishments on Sable Island, from his own perspective.

> *Gentlemen,*
>
> *It is now rather more than eleven years since I went to reside on Sable Island as a Superintendent, leaving a profitable business behind me in Halifax, and at the suggestion of the worthy Commissioner of those days, to endeavour to find out the best method of improving and making the Establishment to become generally useful. I found it in a very inefficient state; I had agreed for one hundred pounds per annum to superintend only, but finding the Establishment utterly destitute of many things that were absolutely necessary, that I applied myself to mechanical labouring, and by the dint of great cautions, I have constructed*

upwards of thirty houses of different sizes, some of them warehouses for the preservation of shipwrecked property after it is saved on the Island. Also eight six-wheel carts, and one four-wheeled wagon. Also a portable wharf of fifty feet long, standing on two pair of wheels, with a capstan to heave it up out of the water, and a house built over it, besides sound copper-fastened boats built on a principal peculiarly adapted to the service of working in the surf on the beaches, two of which boats alone are worth £20.00. Now this has all been done with very little or no expense to the Establishment, and without the assistance of mechanical men of any kind. And in the mean time, we have made several extensive endeavours of the Island for cultivation and other purposes, also having assisted in saving the lives of the crews of nearly forty ships with numerous passengers and baggage, besides other property worth at the lowest estimation seventy thousand pounds, besides raising pork and beef for one half of the consumption of the Establishment, also having picked up the wreck of seven large ships' boats built upon them, and repaired them so that they sold in this market for a considerable sum of money, but of which I did not receive one penny.

Now those very great and long continued exertions, with frequent hair breadth escapes from drowning by being upset in boats, has had a tendency to reduce my vigour considerably, and in a certain degree to injure my constitution. But yet it is by those exertions and those preparations to facilitate the saving of lives and property, that so much has been accomplished, and so few lives lost to what there was formerly, and as I cannot save anything from one hundred pounds per annum to benefit my family, and as I am not making anything by the Establishment, my time and labours appear to me to be literally thrown away, and it will leave me in poverty. I therefore humbly submit the above written statement to the wisdom of your councils, praying you to take them into consideration and endeavour to obtain for me some extra remuneration for those extra services, either out of the money produced by those services or in any other way that you may think most just and proper.

Whilst I remain your faithful and obedient servant,
Joseph Darby
To the Commissioners for the affairs of Sable Island at Halifax
E. Wallace
E. Cunard
Wm. Lawson Jr.
Esquires
Halifax, August 15th 1842

Darby received an answer from the commissioners a few months later:

Answer to Captain Darby's letter dated 15th August 1842
November 12th 1842
Sir,
We have to reply to your letter of the 13th of August last, the content of which we have given due consideration. We are well satisfied that your bad winters have been used for the welfare of the Establishment at all times, and although an addition to your pay had already been made in the shape of a percentage in the proceeds of property saved, yet in consideration of your zeal and uniform attention to your duties as Superintendent, we have taken upon ourselves to increase your salary from £100 to £125 to commence the 1st of January next. We are aware that the percentage on goods saved is uncertain in its amount, and it may according to the number of wrecks on the Island be less or more in one year, and this has led us to be the more willing to make the additions. We have also examined your plan of a life boat, and are willing that you should construct one on the Island, the expense of which is not to cost the Establishment more than £25. Herewith you have a sum for the articles of agreement for the men belonging to the Establishment, which please make use of in future, commencing on the 1st January next, when repaid by the men you can forward

it to Halifax for the signature of the Commissioners.
You will receive by the Sisters *the remainder of the supplies required for the winter.*
We remain, Sir, your obedient servants.

This pay raise came after a busy summer on the island. One of Darby's remaining journals starts on the 1st of July 1842. He writes:

Commences with the wind WSW and fine clear weather. All hands employed overhauling the potatoes, picking the rotten ones out. In the afternoon, I sent two hands down to the East End to help Mr. Adams catch a horse to put in his team. This day ends with the wind and weather the same.

The people of Sable Island were busy farming, making repairs, and scavenging materials from the wrecks of the *Isabell* and *Eliza*. On the 10th of this month, the *Victoria* arrived from Halifax to ship supplies back for auction. "We shipped two large anchors belonging to the *Marmora*, with sundry irons," Darby recalled. "We then towed the vessel down to the wreck of the *Mersey*. We got her two large anchors shipped, and her iron tiller. I sent a boat's crew on board the *Victoria* this evening to go down with her to the *Tanting* where we have a small quantity of *lignum vitia* ready to ship." Adams also reported finding paddles and flotsam belonging to some steam boat, fresh painted red, and made of English elm, suggesting an unseen wreck off the coast of the island.

What Darby calls "lignum vitia" is properly known as *lignum vitae*. This wood is incredibly dense and heavy, and naturally resistant to rot and insect damage. It was prized for shipbuilding and other applications and nearly harvested to extinction at its peak from its native climate in the Caribbean. If *lignum vitae* was washing up on shore or able to be salvaged off wrecks, it would be an extremely valuable find to ship back to Halifax for sale at the maritime auctions. This was a big win for the labourers who were now paid bonuses for their finds.

The *Victoria* took 260 planks of the *lignum vitae*, irons belonging to the *Isabell*, a billet head belonging to the *Triumph*, and another load of plank on board before setting sail to Halifax after a week at Sable Island.

Darby usually sent men to collect materials from wrecks without supervision. Occasionally he would join them to help, which must have been frustrating for the men used to working alone. "I went down to the East End early this morning," Darby wrote on July 22nd. "I found the people at the foot of the lake had given up working at the Brig, and were coming home. I turned them back and we went to the Brig together, where with great endeavours, we got out some more wood by being in the water in the vessels, hold up to the middle. The water is thick black and slimy, and the wood so slimy that it is difficult to hold it, and so imbedded in the sand under water that it is very difficult to get any more of it until the vessel alters her position somehow or other. So we gave it up for the present and I went home after visiting the Eastern Establishment, where all is well."

The month of July saw little action in terms of life-saving activity on Sable Island. Save for the occasional storm, summer tended to have fewer incidents. The people of the island kept themselves busy with farm work and maintenance tasks, always with the goal of preparing for the next winter to come.

August passed largely in the same way. Plank was shipped off the island when vessels arrived to carry it, and boats were repaired up at the main station. While no wrecks were apparent, remnants from ships washed up as they often did: on August 3rd, Darby reported, "I saw something black floating in the water off the North Side and did not know what it was. In the evening I sent one hand down the beach to look for it and he found it a mile from home. He reported it to be an old box with one end out, looking like a box for containing foods with two locks on the side, and some letters I could not make out." These kinds of haunting mementos were constant reminders of the dangers of the sand bars, even in clear weather.

As September rolled in, hay-making and harvesting took priority. Most days Darby reported haymaking as their principal occupation, with occasional ship sightings off shore. "I went to the South Side to look for some good peas to cut, but found none," he reported on September 5th, "they all being destroyed by the caterpillars." Provisions arrived from

Halifax on the *Sisters* the following day, but all other ship sightings were unremarkable until the middle of the month.

Thursday, September 15th

Commences with calm and fine weather. All hands at work at the hay. At 10 AM saw the smoke of a steam ship bearing NW to the Westward of the Island, and at 11 AM lost sight of the smoke bearing about WNW. The ship must have been at a considerable distance as we could not see her hull or spars from an elevation of 120 feet above the level of the sea. She appeared by her smoke to be steering about SW or WSW. We completed two large stacks of hay today, and have got enough. Saw a Schooner off the North Side standing to the Westward, and another standing in for the Island. Three small Nova Scotia vessels fishing for mackerel off the North Side. This day ends with the wind East and moderate, fine weather.

Friday, September 16th

Commences with the wind East with rain and fog alternately. At 7 AM, saw a square rigged vessel off the South Side standing in for the Island about four miles to the Eastward of this. After she came to about three miles of the land, she bore up and run to the Westward, inclining from the land a little, when distant from the flagstaff about 4 or 5 miles. She appeared like a very large and long Barque rigged ship with her main mast gone, and a small jury foremast rigged up, on which was set a small topsail and topgallant sail, she had a jib and flying jib, with a mizen and mizen gaff topsail. She appeared very low in the water, with something bulky on deck amidships, whilst looking at her I could not observe any signal, although she was seen very distinct, but the fog set in and we lost sight of her. In about an hour I saw her again, running to the Westward and partly off the land. We again lost sight of her, and saw her no more. This day ends with the wind East and rain and very thick weather.

Darby's more observational entries are interesting as they show his impressive nautical knowledge and attention to detail. He had the benefit of a spyglass, as these were kept on the island, but the low overall elevation of Sable Island made it difficult to reach a vantage point that would allow a person to see any great distance.

He was probably unaware that the next day on September 17th, a story about him ran in *The Times* newspaper in London, England. It echoed a story from a Halifax paper, reading as follows:

> *DISCOVERY ON SABLE ISLAND*
>
> *The Halifax papers last week publish the following singular discovery: — "The following facts have been made known to us by a gentleman of this city, who has his information from the best authority — viz. Captain Darby, sen., Governor (as he is called) of Sable Island. For the last 25 or 30 years there has been a large mount or pyramid of sand, about 100 feet high, on the island, and not very far from the residence of Captain Darby. The winds for some years have been gradually diminishing its height, and after a severe blow some weeks since it was completely blown away, and, singular to say, a number of small houses, built of the timbers and planks of a vessel, were quite visible. On examination they were found to contain a number of articles of furniture and stores, put up in boxes, which were marked '43d Regiment;' the boxes or cases were perfectly rotten, and would not admit of their being removed. A brass dog-collar was, however, discovered by Captain Darby, with the name of 'Major Elliot, 43d Regiment,' on it, and which Captain Darby brought to the city, and presented to Major Tryon, who belongs to the 43d Regiment." — Halifax Herald. Captain Darby has endorsed this extraordinary announcement. Addressing the editor of the Halifax Herald, on Wednesday, he says, "The houses are appearing at the base of the hill, about two miles long, and 60 or 70 feet high, lying parallel with the south coast of the island, the eastern end of which hill is about 55 feet high, covered with grass and other vegetation, about 33 feet below the surface, and 23 above the level of the sea; these houses appear as the sands wear away with the action of the winds. There*

appeared at times numerous bullets of lead, a great number of military shoes, parts of bales of blankets and cloths, brass points of sword scabbards, beeswax, a small glass convex on both sides, a copper half-penny of George II, dated 1749, some military brass buckles, a great number of brass paper-pins, a very small dog's brass collar, with 'Major Elliot, 43d Regiment,' engraved on it, numerous bones, some whole and some broken, with the scalp of hair and head-dress of a young female, a piece of gold band. There are three buildings, which seem to have been constructed of the fragments of some ship; they are situated about 10 feet apart, in a triangular form, and are 10 to 12 feet square."

Sable Island had a habit of swallowing up structures in its ever-shifting sands. This has since been the fate of the buildings that Darby and the others lived in, too. The discovery of this buried encampment provides a fleeting glimpse into the fates of those that survived wrecking on Sable Island before they built the Humane Establishment. Buildings made from ship fragments indicate a long-term residence on the island, and it is impossible to know whether the survivors were ever rescued.

Another interesting point in this article is the line, "Captain Darby, sen., Governor (as he is called) of Sable Island". They point out that the superintendent is now the 'senior', as by this time his son had also become a captain. However, it's the use of the term 'governor' that stands out — this must have really irked the commissioners. On paper, Darby's position was described as a superintendent. He was an employee of the government, and this was made exceptionally clear in the later letters sent to him by the commissioners. Calling Darby a governor implies a significant degree of power and autonomy, and this raises the question of how his role was perceived by people in Nova Scotia and further abroad. The word is never used in any of Darby's personal documents or letters. He was Joseph Darby, Superintendent, when acting in that capacity, and Captain Joseph Darby for everything else; governor only appeared when others were writing about him. This perception that the superintendent was in a position of power undermined the authority of the commissioners, and they knew it.

Darby's journal entries continued daily for the rest of the month of September. On the 21st, he lamented that he "discovered that the rats were making great havoc amongst our turnips, and we have been obliged to pull them all before they are good for anything". It was a rainy month, and the autumn settled in quickly.

He recorded a strange event on September 22nd. Two of the workers had gone down to the South Side of the island the day before and spent the night. When they returned, they told Darby what they had seen. Darby didn't speculate, but simply recorded what they said.

"They saw a strange and unusual light about two miles to the Westward of the little house where they stopped on the South Side, about the spot where the Schooner *Senator* was cast away. It said to appear above the land about 6 or 8 feet, in a large bright light about the bulk of a large pot, and incline downwards until it touched the land, all the time diminishing in size until it disappeared on the surface of the land. In a few seconds again it would be seen larger and bright above the land, descend slowly, diminishing in size until it was lost sight of on the surface of the land. This was repeated five or six times in the same spot, and within the space of about five minutes. To this James Jackson and Martin Clye are willing to swear."

Terms like "UFO" or "alien" weren't available for use by Darby or his men. Speculation around this event is confined to this entry. Despite his long affiliation with the seafaring world, Darby never betrayed himself as a superstitious man in his writing. Strange occurrences were written as curiosities, rather than as things to be feared.

As September drew to a close, this volume of Darby's journals concluded, and the rest for the year 1842 are lost.

The next year we see greater tensions arise between Darby and the commissioners in their letters. In one case, Darby circumvented the commissioners entirely to address the current lieutenant governor of Nova Scotia, Lucius Bentinck Cary, Viscount Falkland. As Darby explains, he did this because he was missing a paycheck from the previous year.

He first attempts to collect his dues from the commissioners, as seen in this letter from September 1843.

Sable Island, September 3, 1843

Gentlemen,

I received your much respected letter of the 1st of the present month with the Island articles, and I send your copy of the journal up to the 5th of June last. Also enclosed is a memorandum of articles that will be wanting for the ensuing winter.

The man Fisk goes off this time. He has been employed here on the Island since the 20th of June last, at the same rate of wages as the other men. We were one man short when I hired him, and the man John Myers has been sick ever since he came here last, until within the last four days he has gone to work.

Our life boat has been complete for some time past, and I have given W. Duchete an order on you for £25, the amount you promised to assist me to build her, for which I thank you and hope she will be a useful ornament on the Establishment. She is worth between £50 and £60. I have sent W. Duchete some certificate about her for your information.

Our principal working boat that has been in hand service for the last eight years is getting tender and has been a good deal worked with carrying heavy loads. I would recommend having a new one built to supply her place, fearing she might give way suddenly. I will build one this winter on the Island 22 feet long by 7 feet wide, and copper fasten her on the plan that is peculiarly necessary here for the sum of £12,6,0 by having what assistance I can get from the people of the Island.

I am sorry, Gentlemen, that Mr. Duchete has not been able to credit me with 1 1/2 percent on net proceeds of property that went to Halifax the summer of 1842, I received it only on the proceeds of 1841. Also, the premiums for my sons on the wrecks of the Isabell *and the* Louisa, *all previous to the end of 1843. I have to beg, Gentlemen, that you will put those sums in his possession so as to enable him to give me credit for them.*

Whilst I remain your faithful and obedient servant,
Joseph Darby

As this letter did not appear to yield the desired results, Darby decided to move further up the chain of command to write to the lieutenant governor, to whom the commissioners reported, a month later.

> *To the Right Honourable Lucius Bentinck, Viscount Falkland, etc etc etc. Lieutenant Governor and Commander in Chief in and over Her Majesty's Province of Nova Scotia and its Dependencies, etc etc etc.*
> *May it please your Excellency,*
> *To permit me, the undersigned, to present your Excellency with a package of cranberries, the produce of this barren Island, and to state to your Excellency that the Establishment here is at present in a very efficient state, and I humbly beg of your Excellency to grant this humane and beautiful Establishment your protection and support, and to grant me your favour and protection. Also my sons, if they are found worthy, one of which the oldest is in charge of the Revenue Schooner Sisters, and three others are with me here, which with myself are doing all that we can to improve and benefit the Establishment. But I am sorry to inform your Excellency that the small claim I had last year against the Establishment for extraordinary cart work and boat building is not yet liquidated, and as I wish to be guided entirely by your Excellency's will, I cannot take any further step in the claim until I have your entire approbation.*
> *Whilst I most devotedly remain your Excellency's most humble and obedient servant,*
> *Joseph Darby, Superintendent of Sable Island*
> *Sable Island, October 1843*
> *P.S. Will your Excellency please to favour the bearer with an answer.*
> *Claims for boat building and cart making. Has made 9 two-wheel and one 4-wheel wagon. Built 2 large boats, copper fastened, besides repairing 7 or 8 castaways, which were sent to Halifax and sold. Has created more than 30 useful buildings, having been enabled with only a few nails and bricks. Has also*

built a new lifeboat worth £60, for which was promised only £25.

Other problems were beginning to stack up against Darby. The next month, he submitted a report to the commissioners explaining how Americans were behaving aggressively towards the islanders. The Schooner *Alpha* was a particular problem. Being situated in a major nautical thoroughfare, and without any defences either natural or constructed, the people of the island were incredibly vulnerable. The responsibility of ensuring their safety fell to the superintendent, and Darby could only beg for intervention from the commissioners in cases such as this.

Darby took testimonials from the men working on the island to support his own about the *Alpha*. William Myers, James Jackson, Guy Hallett, John Stevens, and Charles Adams all joined the superintendent in accusing the Americans of disturbing the peace on Sable Island.

A report of the aggressions and annoyances made on the British Establishment on Sable Island by American citizens in a Schooner called the Alpha *of Hull over Boston, State of Massachusetts, United States, commanded by Captain Bewse in the year 1842, as follows, viz.:*

William Myers says, I was sent by the Superintendent on the 8th day of August last to the West End of the said Island to look around the shores. That I saw a large American Schooner (which has since learned out to be the Alpha*) laying close in shore off the West End on the North Side abreast of a little inlet from the sea to the lake. A boat belonging to her was laying close into the land wash with two men in her, keeping her afloat whilst five men were on shore with guns, firing at seals. That as soon as they saw me on horse back, they run to their boat and without waiting for her to land, they rushed into the water, hove their game into the boat, and one of them held on to the boat whilst she was pulling off and dragged him through the water some distance in their haste to get away. They went on board, and the vessel soon got under weigh and stood off and was soon out of sight in the fog.*

Signed William Myers
Sworn to before me this 20th day of November 1843 at Sable Island, Joseph Darby, S.O.

James Jackson and Guy Hallett says, that on the 19th of August last, we were sent by the Superintendent to the West End to watch the actions of the crew of the Schooner Alpha *that was then laying close in shore on the North Side, and to prevent them from shooting seals or taking a boat that was placed there in an uninhabited house. When we got near the NW Bar, we saw a boat on shore with six or eight men. They were cutting some iron out of a piece of wreck. We saw where they had dug out a piece of timber and cut three copper bolts out and took away. As soon as they saw us they rushed off and went on board the large Schooner the* Alpha, *as at this time there was a small Schooner in company with her. In about half an hour, the boat returned on shore with four men, two of them armed with percussion guns, loaded as the caps were to be seen on the tubes, and one of them had a pistol or some bulky weapon in his boom. They had shot belts, and carried powder flasks round their bodies, and wadding stuck in their belts. We asked them what they wanted, what was their business here, and what was their names, with the name of their vessel. They told us the vessel was the* Elfee, *the Master was Barras, and she belonged to Barras. They asked us what we were firing at; they thought it was Mexican War on the Island, that the Black Warrior had been taken and Hell kicked up, but guessed the Cutter would not take them. We told them if they were in distress for any thing, to come to headquarters for it, but not to be shooting seals or taking any thing from the shores of the Island. They said that their old fellow (meaning the Master) would not come to headquarters or land on the Island for a hundred dollars, and after a great deal of the like conversation, they went off and we remained at the little house all night to watch their motions. I, Jackson, also say that on the 29th of August last, I saw the Schooner* Alpha *laying within 3/4 of a mile of the shore, taking fish very fast both in the vessel and in her*

boat, which was a short distance from her.
Signed James Jackson
Signed Guy Hallett
Sworn to before me this 20th day of November 1845, Joseph Darby, S.O. at Sable Island

John Stevens says, that I am in charge of an outport on Sable Island at the East End of the lake. That five men came on shore from the Schooner Alpha *on the 12th of September last, where the wreck of the ship* Eagle *had just gone to pieces. Two of them landed, one with an ax, the other with a club, which he was swinging about at a furious rate when I came on the beach. I asked them what they wanted, they said they were looking for a gas, spoke a great deal of that ballahoo of a Steamer coming to take them and firing at them, but that they had guns would be heard as far as hers, and 15 or 16 able bodied men well prepared for defence, and would not be taken very easily. I also saw where they had cut or knocked out some copper spikes on the North Side, near the wreck of* Tanting.
Signed John Stevens
Sworn to before me this 20th day of November 1843 at Sable Island, Joseph Darby S.O.

Charles Adams says, that I am in charge of an outpost on Sable Island near the East End. That on the 9th day of August last, there were three American Schooners laying off the North Side. The crews of one of them came to my house, I think they were from the Alpha. *I asked them the name of their vessel, and the Master's name. The man that spoke said his vessel had no name, and for his name when he was at home, they called him William Bell or Jack, that he supposed the Englishmen thought themselves very cunning about the Island, and gave no other information about themselves. They frequently land and shoot seals and brawl about the shores of the Island a great deal, that some time after this part of the crew of the* Alpha *came to my house, the Master gave his name Bewse, and the name of the vessel the* Alpha *of Hull near Boston. Told me if I had all the fish that they had caught here, over three hundred barrels, I would have a good summer's work that he knew that Steamer came on purpose to take him, that he expected nothing due but to be taken when he saw her, but on a second thought he would jump the Schooner over the dry bar before he would be taken inside of the limits, that he considered himself a lucky man and would say it again next year. He offered me two dollars to go to the West End and get him some butter, which I declined, telling him I knew he could not get any there, which he did not seem willing to believe, and I thought that his object was to get me from home, and then to steal the boat or something else. He also said that if a wreck had happened while he was here, I would have seen fun, for they would have had a load out of her and taken it to Boston.*

Signed Charles Adams

Sworn to before me this 20th day of November 1843 at Sable Island, Joseph Darby S.O.

Joseph Darby says, that I am the Superintendent of Sable Island, and that on the 19th of August last, I sent five men to watch the motions of the Schooner Alpha that was then laying off the North Side near the West End, distant from headquarters about five miles. That the two men stayed up there all night, and on the morning of the 20th, came home and made the subjoined report, that the Schooner also came close and anchored, the Master and four men came on shore. The Master told me that my people told him last night that he must come down and see me and ask me what I wanted with him. He said he belonged to Barnstable, and had sailed out at Boston, but he neither told me his name or vessel's name. I told him I had nothing at all to do with him, was sorry to have to forbid him from shooting seals or committing any kind of depredations about the Island, and particularly the sending armed men on shore to put the isolated inhabitants in bodily fear. That for the fisheries, I did not know much about *them, but that a vessel had been seized here for fishing contrary to treaty. He answered that we had nothing to protect us here, that it was the man's own fault, and that he would take care and he went off. This was the only time that I saw him, a man about 40 or 45 years of age, about 5 feet 7 inches high, round features, a little corpulent, talks quick. The Schooner about 80 or 100 tons with a high main top mast, appears to hake forward, a black looking hull with some kind of a head, carries a boat on the stern, sails great peak to them, flying jib appears to hoist high above the standing jib. On the 14*th *of September, the* Alpha *ran up the South Side from the Eastward and anchored off the wreck of the* Glasgow *where she laid all night, the wind off shore and the sea very smooth. On the morning of the 15*th *about sunrise, it being very calm and smooth, I saw the* Alpha *hauled in stern foremast with her main sail set close in to the wreck of the* Glasgow, *so close that the South Beach hid the hull of the vessel from my view, distant about five miles. I suspected he was after some mischief, I got my horse immediately and went up, but whilst I was wading across the lake, distant from him about five miles, the Schooner moved out, and with a light air of wind, run off about 3/4 of a mile and anchored. The South Beach hid their operations from my view, but when I got up to the wreck, I saw that one of her anchors that lay on a piece of deck forward under the windlass was gone. It was an iron stocked anchor, about 14 or 15 cust. wt., and it was plain to be seen laying there a few days ago. The ship's rail and bulwark abreast of where the anchor lay had been sawed down to the deck the evening before, and it was floated on shore on the beach, with many fresh cuts and chips, and it appeared as if every impediment had been removed the evening before so as to take the advantage of high water and smooth sea in the morning early to haul the Schooner in, and with their tackles ready, swing it off in a few minutes. The Schooner still had the tackles up between her masts, had her boat out alongside, and whilst I was standing on the beach looking at them, they hoisted up their boat to the stern and got under weigh. I had been very uneasy about this vessel and crew ever since she has been about here. We have herded our cattle every night for some time, for fear they would find them at some distance from home and destroy them, and if they have not got much from the shores, it is because we have not left much for them to get. Several other vessels have been about the Island, but we have had no reason to complain of any of them. They have all been very curt and well behaved, except the crew of the vessel above mentioned, which has not since been seen.*

Signed Joseph Darby, Sable Island, November 20th 1843

The commissioners received this report from Darby, but offered no direct solutions to the threat against the island. Instead, they identified another problem: the Schooner *Sisters* that serviced the island was getting old, and needed to be replaced. They sent the following letter to the office of the lieutenant governor in response.

Halifax, 22 January 1844
Sir,
We have the honour to enclose herewith for the information of His Excellency the Lieutenant Governor, a report from Mr. Joseph Darby, the Superintendent of Sable Island, relative to the conduct of the crews of American fishing vessels during the past years - the report is accompanied by the affidavit of several men belonging to the Establishment.

We beg to remark that the visits of American vessels for the purpose of fishing near the Island are becoming every year more frequent.

The Schooner Sisters, *having been found not to possess the qualities required for the previous services in which she has been employed, we have in contemplation, should it meet the approbation of His Excellency, to dispose of her, and to build or purchase another, more efficient vessel. The funds at the disposal of the Commissioners are sufficiently ample to justify this expenditure.*

We have the honour to be, sir, your most obedient servants.

> E. Wallace
> E. Cunard
> W. Lawson Junior
> Commissioners for Sable Island
> To the Honorable Sir R.D. George

The easy problems were solved with money. The harder ones were left up to Darby. He also contributed more to the island than just manual labour and management: he created resources, such as a thorough catalogue of wrecks and lives and property saved from between the years 1802 to the time of writing, in 1844. This appears to have been done, on the one hand, for the benefit of the establishment and the commissioner's documentation. On the other hand, as we see in the following letter, he also used it to demonstrate the labours done by the island employees. As always, Darby was working in both his own and the establishment's interest.

> *Sable Island, November 30th 1844*
> *Honourable Sir,*
> *I humbly beg leave to intrude upon your kindness to trouble you with the care of two lists for His Excellency, the Commander in Chief; one is a general list of wrecks with names and dates since the year 1802 up to the present date. The other is a list of wrecks with the lives and property saved, and with the improvements on Sable Island, for five periods of seven years each, commencing with my copies of which I have sent to the Commissioners, and I am very desirous first to obtain your Honour's favourable opinion of those proceedings, and on presenting them to His Excellency, to represent this Establishment, His Excellency's patronage, and favour of which I hope it is deserving from its beauty, order, and usefulness.*
> *And sir, if you please to look at these lists, you will see something near to what extent my services has been unremunerated, as there is nothing exaggerated, but the nominations are rather under than exceeding the real amounts and valuations. But the*

same motives prompt me still which did at the first, and so I am yet about to labour, nothing shall remain wanting that I can do, hoping through the kind influence of his Excellency, that the Government will consider me at last, and will not take so much mechanical labour from an individual without remunerating him for it.

With sentiments of the most profound respect and veneration for your Honourable person, I remain most devotedly your obedient servant,
Joseph Darby
To the Honorable Sir RD George, Baronet
Halifax, NS

Darby continued the trend of circumnavigating the commissioners in another letter, regarding his views on the frequency of visitation to the island by ships from Halifax. This came after the wreck of the *Saladin*, a much discussed shipwreck at the time. The *Saladin* was a Barque built in Newcastle, England, and was sailing to London from Valparaíso, Chile. On May 21st of 1844, this ship became stranded on Harbour Island, near Country Harbour.

According to reports, the *Saladin* carried a valuable cargo including guano, 90 tons of copper, and silver bars and coins. A man named Fielding had become a passenger on this ship after escaping from a Peruvian prison, and motivated by the valuable cargo, he turned the crew and officers against each other. His plans went awry as the mutineers killed the captain and the officers, and then Fielding and his son. Some level of forethought might have revealed the flaw in this plan, as with no navigators left, the ship wrecked on Harbour Island. The mutinous crew were tried in the last piracy trial in Nova Scotia's history, and the cargo was lost.

This incident was of great concern to the Nova Scotian government, but even more to Darby. The *Saladin* could have just as easily wrecked on Sable Island, and he could have been invaded by pirates with no qualms about murder. He had already dealt with violent threats and dangerous survivors of other wrecks, but the *Saladin* incident must have been a realisation of Darby's greatest security fears.

> *Sable Island, July 3rd, 1844*
> *Most Honorable Sir,*
> *In contemplating on the awful occurrence of the wreck of the* Saladin *on the coast of Nova Scotia and all the circumstances connected with it, being me to the conclusion that we have great reason here to require, at the merciful interference of Providence that has directed her course clear of this place, by which means the guilty perpetration of such horrible murders, I hope and trust will be brought to punishment.*
> *Now, much Honoured Sir, had that ship come here, she would probably have taken ground so far off that a boat would very seldom approach her from the shore of the Island, on account of the breakers between the wreck and the shore, and as we have seen this spring that a week has not passed without some one of the American fishermen standing in for the Island, and literally running along shore all round it to see if there was any thing now on shore. Some of the vessels have a crew of twenty men or upwards on board, and are prepared for plundering as well as fishing, and had they found a wreck here of that description, they would never have left her whilst there was any thing to be plundered worth a cent. And they might frequently communicate with the wreck from the sea, when we could not approach her from the shore, and with the mutual assistance that they would have received from the crew, it would have been utterly beyond the strength of the Establishment to have resisted them, or even, I am afraid, to have protected ourselves. And it would have completely facilitated the escape of the guilty crews from justice, the melancholy circumstances that might have attended it, your Honour can better conceive than I can describe. And I hope that it will have that effect on His Excellency through your kind representation to convince him of the propriety of ordering the Government Schooner* Sisters *to visit the Establishment more frequently during the summer season, and whilst it is surrounded by such bold and troublesome neighbours*

as the American fishermen, two months without a visit is a long time, as one wreck might produce more disastrous effects than many years could make good, and generally evil is easier prevented than remedied.

And I remain your Honour's most humble and obedient servant,

Joseph Darby, Superintendent of Sable Island
To the Honorable Sir R.D. George, Baronet. Halifax, N.S.

Despite his many pleas for assistance, little change came to Sable Island during Darby's residence as superintendent. It was up to him to decide how to protect the people of the island, how to distribute their unpredictable rations, and how to distribute the labour amongst those sent to him from Halifax.

Darby's entire collection of journals for the year of 1845 is preserved. The year began with a holiday, followed by the renewal of contracts for those employed on the island. "The men all signed the articles today for another year except John Clybourne and Guy Hallett," writes Darby on January 2nd, "who have given notice to leave in three months." Stevens and Adams, the men supervising the other outposts on the island, signed on for another two years each.

January was spent chopping wood, hunting seals, and scavenging materials from wrecks of the *Bob-Logie*, the *Glasgow*, and the *Maria* as they were pushed out of the sand by the shifting tides. "Always find that when there is but little to do, that it is more difficult to divide that little that all hands may take an equal part of it," Darby wrote, "than when there is plenty to do and every body has to work hard." He distributed the rations, but they were thin as always in the slow winter months, and the men complained about them often.

The rations they received were not always of an acceptable quality. Spoiled barrels of pickled fish, rancid preserves, and mouldy bread were sometimes returned to Halifax, and other times simply discarded for the cost of shipping it back. In February, Adams came up to the main station to discuss the coffee he had received. "Adams brought up a small bag of small stones, which he says he picked out of the last quarter's coffee that he had. The quantity that he picked out of them was about 8 pounds, I weighed the stones and they weighed rather above 3/4 a pound. Stevens had them bring up a similar quantity of stones which he says that he picked out of about the same quantity of coffee, and we have found a larger proportion of stones in what we have used here, they having settled towards the bottom of the cask. This is the coffee was sent here in the Spring of 1844." Somewhere along the line, the suppliers for the island were cheating by mixing stones with the coffee beans.

On February 18th, an accident took place in the lumber yard. It serves as a stark reminder of the dangers of injury or illness on the island, as it was the superintendent and his family who were responsible for tending to the unwell. "One of the men whilst chopping or working with some wood on the yard got cut by accident from an axe that another man was using. It fell with such weight and force across his foot near the toes that I fear two of them are cut right through bones, sinews and all, and two of the others much cut. We had some difficulty to stop the blood, and had to watch him all night in which he laid in great agony."

The following day, "the man with his cut foot has not stirred off his back all night where he was laid before the fire, but he is in less agony today than he was. We have not opened the wound yet to dress it for fear of its breaking out to bleed, but I have removed the tourniquet from the ankle which eases him much."

A few days later, a ship arrived on the island. Darby had a brief visit with his son Edward, which sounded like a highlight of the season. On February 21st, Darby recorded that "at about one o'clock, my son Edward came to the house before we saw or knew anything of him. He said he had landed from his vessel at the West End and walked down in company with Mr. Pike, who he had out walked, and left behind a distance of 1 1/2 miles. I sent a man with a horse to meet him. My son told me that as the wind was a head, they had made the land at the West End and found the sea smooth, and to make the most of the day, he landed up there and walked down. And as the weather was thick he had directed the people to work the vessel down with short tacks in shore, and by the time that the vessel got down he was ready to start again. I got out a boat, got a cask of water and some fuel, and put him on board, and at 3 PM he sailed for

Halifax."

The injured man didn't leave for Halifax with Edward, instead waiting out his injury on the island. Had he left, he would have forfeited his position on Sable, and lost his steady, if modest, income. "The man that has his foot cut is very bad," Darby remarked in his journal by the end of February.

As hard as the winter was on the people living on the island, it was even more difficult for the animals brought from across the ocean. The wild horses had long since adapted to the winter, feeding on whatever wild peas and grasses stuck up through the snow, and the domestic horses were often set free to live among these hardier creatures for the season. "Some of our cattle look sick," Darby wrote on March 4th, "and will not eat either hay, oats, turnips, potatoes, oatmeal, or anything. One cow had a dead calf today which was opened. Found its guts growing to the liver, and the liver and gall as large as a beast of five years old should be in a healthy state."

By the 10th of March, the injured man was still laid up but had recovered enough to set about working from inside the house. "He is picking oakum," Darby noted in his journal. Picking oakum meant unravelling bits of rope so the fibre could be used for other purposes. It was a tedious and manually taxing job, usually reserved as a punishment for sailors on ships, but one that could be done without moving around. Being able to contribute in this way meant that the injured man was technically working, and wouldn't have to lose his pay any longer than necessary.

The rest of the workers on the island were being productive, even without farm work or shipwrecks to attend to. "We have now sawed 6600 feet of lumber, and made 33 thousand shingles," Darby reported mid-March. The days passed routinely, and they got a holiday for Easter. Darby mused over the skies in his journal on Easter Day. "The moon rose this evening perfectly clear and full at the time of the sun's setting, or 4 or 5 minutes after, and I am of the opinion that the moon was at the full today instead of yesterday, as yestereven she rose more than an hour before the sun set, and her orb was a little elongated, and had not apparently come to the full, which is contrary to the rules presiding Easter."

The journal for the second quarter of the 1845 begins with occasional April snows, and the discovery that the potatoes they had buried in the ground for the winter had kept very well and were good to eat. "The people have been looking round the Island a little today," Darby reported near the end of April, "but it is rather difficult to find full employment for them at present, as our working cattle is rather weak to go collecting firewood yet, and I am afraid to work them down too low for fear in case of a wreck, they would not be able to do the necessary work."

On April 27th, a few hours after dawn, the schooner *Sylph* and Captain Young of the Revenue Service stopped at Sable Island on a cruise and on her way to Halifax. "My son John Henry returned to the Island, and Guy Hallett and John Clybourne left the Island." These two departing men had reached the end of their contracts. In a rare mention of his other family members, Darby noted that "my wife and two children went to Halifax in this vessel on account of ill health." They would remain in Halifax for some time.

As the weather warmed up, Darby moved his household from their winter station to the New House, a breezier structure for the season. "Six fine half-grown pigs took fits yesterday altogether, and this morning four of them are dead," Darby reported. A few days later, he notes: "yesterday, William Myers gave in notice to leave the Island in three months in a very insolent manner because I was obliged to speak sharp to him on account of his great neglect of the animals in his care. By which neglect we have lost several fine young hogs, and indeed I have always had a great deal of trouble with him to make him take care of the cattle, and I will have to turn him into the boat and get some other person to attend the stock." As these journals were periodically sent to the commissioners to account for the daily affairs of the island, Darby was careful to record his account of events like this.

"At sunrise this morning, the eclipse was to be seen distinct and beautiful, and continued until near 6 o'clock," Darby wrote on May 6th. "We gathered in all our domestic horses today and trimmed their feet, manes, and tails. We put in about a cart load of hay from the stack into the barn. The grass is so very backward that we must hay our cattle in and feed them. The mackerel gulls made their first appearance today, an indicator of a backward spring." The people of the island were reliant on these natural signs of seasonal change to guide their activity, particularly with respect to the animals in their care.

Occasionally ships came close to wrecking on the island, but managed to get themselves out of danger. On May 12th, Adams came to the main station to report a sighting on the afternoon of May 3rd. "He saw a large ship on the NE Bar about 1 1/2 miles from the point. The sails were partly levied up, her head to the Northward, her stern apparently very much elevated, and her bow depressed, the sea at times appeared to break all over her. He got his horse and rode down to the bar as fast as he could, and when he got within a mile of the point, the ship appeared to move ahead and finally passed over the bar into deep water on the North Side, when he steered first to the Northward and then to the NE until out of sight, and that he saw her on the bar for the space of two hours, and does not know how long she might have been there before he saw her."

As the weather became nicer, they spotted more ships from the island. Darby reported several schooners on both sides of the island, and on the 14th one anchored. "Two Schooners in sight off the South Side, a Schooner bearing NW, steering for the flag staff. She stood and anchored in 2 fathoms of water, and the Master and six men came on shore. They report the Schooner the *Two Sisters* of Beverly NJ, 11 days out on a banking voyage. Found fish scarce to the Westward of the Island and was going to Banquereau, and from that to the Green Bank."

When the ground could be tilled, farming concerns took over, as this was the only source of fresh produce for the people of Sable to eat. Potatoes, beets, carrots, and cabbages were all grown with varying levels of success each year. Eggs were another source of fresh food this time of year, if they could find nests hidden around the island. Provisions arrived on Edward Darby's ship near the end of May in a great bank of fog, and they shipped out four barrels of skins and two casks of seal oil for Halifax.

Part of the summer work was looking after the horses, both wild and domestic. Adams' horses had vermin and he treated them with some mercurial ointment. Veterinary care for these animals was done by whoever was available. "I sent one hand to the East End to help Adams and Stevens to catch and cut some young horses that were troublesome about the fences," Darby wrote on June 3rd, "and to bleed one of his work horses that is sick." When this was done, the same men were then tasked with caulking and repairing a scow to transport wood. The work was varied and shared among all.

The scow was an imperfect solution for transporting wood across the large lake that sat in the middle of the island. Darby would take this boat with his men and two teams a few miles away for wood, but "having loaded the Scow pretty deep, and there was a less of a swell in the Lake, we had to throw part of the load overboard in the middle of the Lake to keep the Scow from filling with water." The next day, all hands were employed hauling up the wood from the scow, and gathering up what had been thrown overboard the day before, it having drifted on shore.

To make this job easier, Darby planned to build a substantial bridge into the lake from the bank to where a boat could reach. "This distance, which is about 300 yards, has from 2 to 14 inches of water over it and we cannot communicate with a boat in the lake without being continually wet," he said. It was eventually decided another 80 yards should be added to this. The rest of June was spent building this bridge, gardening, fishing, and hunting wild duck eggs, "from which source we derive a great deal of food during this month."

In the third quarter of 1845, a small Schooner arrived. "At 9 AM she anchored," Darby wrote on July 7th. "I sent a boat on board and found her to be the Schooner *Pilot*, Laybold Master, from Halifax, come for a load of horses. I immediately made preparations for catching some as at present there is a number about the lake that are rather an encumbrance on the pasture at the spot." These horses, once shipped to Halifax, were sold at auction, and often ended up working in the mines in Cape Breton. Their strength and small stature made them ideal for the narrow working conditions there.

"The people came up early this morning from the East End with some horses," the following day, "which we got into the pound and we got a large set from the Westward, out of which we picked fifteen head of the best and got them shipped with fodder and water." The *Pilot* set sail for Halifax with its unhappy cargo. Now low on penned horses, Darby had more rounded up. "We had three hound horses shut up in the pound all night which were caught this morning and altered, and put them in the pasture so that we can attend them until they got well."

They saw other ships off shore. The Schooner *Union*, Captain Bremner from Lunenburg, appeared nearby on a mackerel fishing voyage, and spent a few days circling the island. Darby sent a boat on board to find out if they had caught any fish, but they hadn't had a bite from any mackerel.

In late July, the superintendent decided on two new buildings they would construct. "I commenced building a shed on the North Beach to shelter our working boats in during the summer season," he wrote on July 19th, "and to have them near the water when they are wanting, as it would not do to leave them exposed on the hot sand." It took all hands three days to construct this shelter, in addition to performing their regular duties. Next, they "commenced building a new watch house on the hill, the old one not being worth repairing."

They worked on this house as mackerel season continued around them. A Schooner named the *Gentile* of Plymouth anchored nearby on July 30th, Captain Atwood coming ashore to report they were 14 days out on their mackerel fishing voyage. The next day, as the people were employed removing the old rotten platform from the house on the hill and laying a new one, the Schooner *Pilot* anchored again. This time, it was on a mackerel voyage, and its Captain Rogers came on shore. He asked if he could put some barrels of salt on shore of Sable Island to get them out of the way for a short time. "As we were entirely out of salt on the Island, I thought it a good opportunity to get a supply," Darby decided, "and took ten barrels for the use of the Island, which I gave him a receipt for, intending that the owner should be paid by the Commissioners in Halifax."

The mackerel fishermen treated Sable Island as a rest stop, occasionally coming on shore. Darby seemed to have been happy for the occasional company of seafaring folk, having spent the first few decades of his life at sea himself. Captain Bremner stopped by at the beginning of August, and the Schooner *Daring* appeared a few days later with a delivery of flour and some visitors, Mr. T. Humphrey and Mr. Monk. It wasn't unusual that people would accompany the supplies ships in the summer months for a look at Sable Island. The Island had a reputation on the mainland, and people were curious. Captain Bremner stopped by before leaving the area after finding no fish, going to try the continent. He told Darby that the *Loring* had gone too, but this ship and the Pink *Adams* landed their crews on Sable Island a few days later for a brief time. It was a busy summer filled with visitors.

Though the weather was good for sailing and supply ships were able to make the trip easily, this did not mean that the supplies that came from the mainland were significantly improved. On August 13th, Darby "sent two hands with the wagon down to the Eastward again for another load of mixed fodder, the others employed in the store overhauling and repacking the meat, and otherwise washing out the store and washing the barrels to cool them. Adams came up this forenoon for some meat, he brought some meat with him that he had got here but a short time ago and says that it is so bad that he cannot eat it. I see nothing the matter with it and it is precisely the same as what we are now using here, and I had to give him more of the same kind." Whether the meat was good or bad, it was all they had on hand.

As August turned into September, the main concern was gathering hay for the animals over winter. The fodder was stacked in large piles, referred to as cocks of hay, and if it rained before they could stack it the hay would have to be spread out and dried again on the next clear day. On September 3rd, "we commenced hauling up our hay, we got about half of it in the barn and the remainder in a cock when it began to rain. Captain Bremner came to an anchor here today. He came on shore and said he was getting short of bread, wished to know if I could spare him a little, or else he would have to give his voyage up and he had done nothing as yet but wished to remain a little longer." Not wishing to let Bremner down, and thinking of the supplies the island needed, Darby decided to help. "I had some bread that had come out of the ship *Eagle* in 1843, some of it was good, and some that had been wet was moulding. We picked it all over, took what was bad out, and the remainder was about 2 1/2 barrels. He was glad to take, for which he gave me good herring and halibut in full value for." Darby did the same for other ships, occasionally.

In mid-September, Captain Rogers of the Schooner *Pilot* came to collect the barrels of salt he had left on shore. "The sea being rather bad, he could not ship them in his own boat, and we assisted him with one of our boats to ship his barrels and get some water, and by him I sent letters to Halifax with the list for the fall supplies to the Commissioners with some empty packages to be filled, and the Schooner sailed for Halifax with between 4 and 5 barrels of fish, which appears to be very scarce about the Island this season. I got a barrel of salt fish from Captain Rogers in lieu of a few pieces of meat I gave him." Captain Loring came a few days later to get water, "and reports being short of provisions, requested me to let him have a barrel of flour, which I did for 30 shillings, on which he paid me four dollars, and promised to pay the remainder the next time he came on shore. Note this barrel of flour I must replace to the Island first opportunity."

These interactions with fishing vessels were outside of Darby's job description. Later in his career, the commissioners would take issue with these trades and deals that they had not sanctioned, presuming that Darby had done so in order to make himself a profit. It's impossible to know of any details from these meetings that Darby did not record in his journals. But for those that were recorded, they appear to have been done in recognition of the need for cooperation between people caught so far from the mainland. His trades, as far as they are recorded, sound to be fair deals.

Storm season came in the fall, and Darby recorded some days of heavy weather.

Wednesday, September 24th

Commences with the wind ESE, and at 4 AM there was some very heavy squalls. I got up and made a light and called up all hands to look after our boats in the lake. We found them all riding very well. It was moonlight, and one hand waded in and made a long rope fast to one at a time, and by the bridge we hauled them until they took the ground and we secured them well. At day light the squalls were violent, but by sun rise the wind fell suddenly. I

ISLAND MANAGEMENT

took a horse and went to the West End where I saw Loring laying off the West End house on the South Side riding very well. Adams was about three miles to leeward under close reefs beating up, and Bremner was to anchor about four miles West of the West head. The wind blowed the tops of all our hay stacks. In the afternoon, the wind hauled to the SSE and the vessels came round the NW bar to the North Side. This day ends with the wind SSE and dark moderate weather.

When the weather took these sorts of turns, Darby was braced for the worst. There were still many fishing vessels in the nearby waters. The bad weather continued into the following day, but no wrecks took place.

Thursday, September 25th
Commences with the wind WNW and moderate dark weather. I sent two teams and some hands to the West End to haul home a stack of hay that was blown down and to repair the tops of two others. Two hands went to the South Side to put the stack of hay to rights that is over there, and we put up some fence that was blown down. At 10 AM, saw a lofty Barque rigged ship off the South Side standing in for the Island, but when at a distance of 15 or 16 miles, she wore round and stood to the Southward. The three fishing Schooners crossed the NW bar again this morning and rain down the South Side to the Eastward. This day ends with the wind NE and fine weather.

On the 27th, Captain Bremner came on shore to collect some firewood. Darby went out and spoke with him, and learned that they had felt the gale on the 24th very heavily but had not suffered loss. He said that Captain Adams lost both anchors, but that they had now found fish on the South Side of the island. He had gotten fourteen barrels in that week alone, a huge improvement from the scarcity earlier in the season. John Stevens came up from the East End later, reporting what Darby had already learned about the storm, and that Loring and Adams had both left for Halifax. The wife and two children of Charles Adams (the island employee) had gone with them to the city.

The fourth quarter of the year 1845 began in October, and on the 5th Captain Bremner turned up again, looking for provisions. "Captain Bremner stated that he had expended all his bread, that he had done very little as yet with catching fish, that now he could get some on the South Side if he could remain, which he could not do without I could spare him a little bread to enable him to remain about the Island a few days longer. It seemed hard to refuse a good man in distress and I let him have two barrels of navy bread and one barrel of potatoes for which he paid one in mackerel, but as this fish is too high and valuable to keep for food on the Island, I will turn it into money and replace the bread on the Island or pay for it the first opportunity that presents itself."

On October 11th, Charles Adams came up to the main station. "Last night Adams came up and reports himself very ill," Darby wrote the following morning. "He remained here all night, and I attended him during the night and gave him something that done him a little good. This morning I sent a man home with him to help put his house in order, and to bring him and his child up here, as he is too ill to be left there alone and I cannot spare a man from the boats crews to stop with him." Adams' wife and other children had just departed for the mainland a short time ago, and there was no one else to look after him. That same day, Darby wrote that "Captain Bremner called here this morning to bid me goodbye and to say he was going to leave the Island and go to the coast of Cape Breton and try for fish along the coast homewards, that he caught thirteen barrels during the last week, and that Loring told him he had caught fifteen barrels, and that both the other vessels left the Island last night for the coast of Cape Breton as the fish here did not appear to be plenty enough to remain longer after them.

"When Captain Bremner was leaving he told me that his pilot had told him that our Adams had been guilty of a misdemeanour, and from the nature of it I was immediately able to convince Captain Bremner that it was not true. I then sent him on board his vessel in our boat. When he got on board he had some private conversation with his pilot and he then called my son and told him to tell me that it was not Adams but Stevens. The boat came on shore and the vessel got under weigh and left the Island, and I had no opportunity to confute this statement, which is also false."

Though he could be critical of the men on the island personally, Darby took great issue with accusations against them by others. The following day, he went down to the West of the Lake to find Stevens and inform him of this circumstance. "He denies most solemnly, and I am satisfied that it is not true," Darby wrote. John Stevens was Darby's brother-in-law, so he may have been more inclined to believe him from the start, but the matter was dismissed.

On the road to find Stevens, Darby came across Adams and the man who was moving him into the main house. "Adams says he is very ill, but he is so much in the habit of romanticizing that I am afraid to depend on all he says," said Darby. "He has shut up one part of the house where his own little things are, and the other parts of the house are ready to be occupied by any persons in distress, and I have directed Stevens to visit that part of the Island occasionally in thick weather." Darby made sure to clarify to whoever read this journal that he had thought everything through and ensured that even after relocating Adams, there was room for others in the main house, and that Adams' post would not go unwatched.

A ship arrived on October 27th, but the weather became rough and they could not unload its cargo. Darby ordered a light hoisted on the flagstaff which they attended all night, mindful of the risk of disorientating any vessel that came too close in the storm. In the morning the weather was clear and they landed the provisions. They shipped off some berries and Charles Adams, his illness having lasted more than a fortnight by this time.

The people of the island were busy storing their food, harvesting barrels of potatoes and other produce, and washing out and storing boats. As the East End Station was now vacant with Adams gone, Darby sent men down to collect the animals and food left there. Bad weather was becoming more frequent, and a heavy gale and rain squalls on November 11th sent all hands out to look for wrecks. Finding none, they set about repairing fences, replacing shingles on the barn, and fixing sundry other things that the storm had damaged.

By November 24th, Darby reports they were entirely out of meat.

He had the people kill an ox to tide them over, which was necessary though it would diminish their ability to work with heavy loads. Some of the pickled fish that they had received in their last shipment from Halifax was so bad that they could not eat them, and they were becoming desperate for protein-rich foods.

Darby recorded an unusual sight on the 25th of November. "Last night a singular phenomena appeared on the South Side, the sea being very heavy and the night very dark. A breaking of the sea would exhibit at intervals of some five or ten minutes a phosphorus light. In some places it could be seen through the gulches on the South Side like a bright light, and at other places where the beach was low and the sea would break high, it would rise with a great bright light to the height of fifteen or twenty feet, like an immense fire, and yet it could only be seen in certain spots at a time."

Like with other strange phenomena on the island, Darby does not speculate as to the cause of the unusual sight. What he saw was likely bioluminescent algae, which appears around other parts of Nova Scotia, such as in the waters of Ship Harbour to the East of Halifax.

If Darby took the sight to be a portent of anything, it must have been ominous. Though they distributed the ox meat among the various stations on the island, they pulled turnips, carrots, and beets from the gardens and found them to be very poor. A barrel of apples was found on the beach, but they were all ground up to mush. Two of the hands were instructed to scavenge the beaches on the South Side for clams which had washed up on shore. It began to rain nearly every day, and one of their boats was wrecked against the shore of the lake. The milk cows were moved into the stables for the winter for protection, as they couldn't risk anything happening to these animals.

In early December, they began hunting ducks, and killed two fat wild horses to eat. The decision to start eating the wild horses was always a red flag that provisions were scarce on the island. On December 12th they decided to kill the hogs, which were five in number and weighed 1000 lbs.

As they whittled down the number of animals, they eventually turned to one of the cows in a disturbing episode. "We killed an old cow today, she is very fat and has been with calf nearly three years," Darby wrote. "The calf was yet in her, preserved and hard, and quite perfect about one foot long with the after cleaning attached to it a little decayed." The hogs were cut up and salted, and cranberries were packed in straw to keep them from freezing too badly.

December continued to be cold and wet. "The shingling on the roof of the barn has got so loose and bad that every strong breeze of wind blows more or less of them off, and the rain yesterday has come down through a bulk of hay 15 or 20 feet thick and wet a great deal of it," Darby lamented on the 17th, "and we are trying to repair it a little today as far as our nails will go."

Christmas came and went with a great snowstorm. The employees were busy washing and cleaning up the old house to move back into for the winter, fitting it with a new stovepipe and other accommodations to make it warmer. As the year ended and they settled into place, Darby finished his journal. "Thus ends the year 1845, and I pray to god that he will bless our friends, and pardon and forgive our enemies, and turn their hearts. J Darby." There were no shipwrecks recorded for the year.

The journals for the months of January to June of 1846 are lost, but a volume containing the entries from the 1st of July to the 30th of September of that year has survived. The entries here, up until the 19th of July, are written by someone other than Darby. This was one of the infrequent occasions when Darby left the island to visit Halifax. There is no indication as to who took over during his absence, but it would be a reasonable guess that one of his sons filled in the logbook in his absence.

Just a few months prior to the start of this next journal, John Hodgson, the son of the previous superintendent, sent a letter to Edward Wallace, the chair of the commissioners. From this letter it seems there was a rumour circulating that Darby was leaving his job, though there is no hint of this in anything preserved from Darby himself. As the Hodgsons had originally wished to keep the control of Sable Island in the family in 1830, it isn't surprising that John took an opportunity to offer himself for the job. Hodgson was residing in Country Harbour at the time, having left his service on the island sometime in the last few years.

Country Harbour
March 20th, 1846
   Dear Sir,
   Hearing that Mr Darby is to leave the Sable Island this season and take up his abode in some other quarter, I now humbly address a few lines to you, informing you that I have been given to understand that if possible I should take charge of the Island after Mr. Darby leaves it. Will you have the kindness to inform me as early as possible after the receipt of this, whether the report respecting Mr. Darby's leaving the Island is true, and if it is, will you have the kindness to use your influence on my behalf. Knowing as you do my personal character and also of my long acquaintance with the Island, having laboured under my father and Mr. Darby for a number of years. And now if the office is to be bestowed upon another, I think an old and experienced hand would be the best person to have the charge thereof. However, I need not say anything further than this. If it is to be given to another, will you be so kind as to let me know the particulars respecting it and also, if you will remember my application, and use your endeavours to procure me the situation and if so I trust you, and the commissioners acting with you, will ever have the cause to repent of the same.
   Wishing you and yours every happiness that this world can afford.
   I remain, Sir, your most obedient humble servant.
   John Hodgson
   Edward Wallace Esq., Halifax

As Darby did not leave the island until 1848, it would seem that John Hodgson's informants were mistaken. His entitlement to the role of superintendent did not ultimately reward him, as Darby was replaced by Matthew McKenna instead of Hodgson.

We pick up Darby's journal again on the 1st of July 1846. The people of the island somehow survived the lean winter of the previous year, and were one again engaged in their summer pursuits. Darby records their business chopping wood, hilling potatoes, hunting ducks, and cleaning out the houses.

On the 19th of July, a new employee came to the island.

Sunday, July 19th

Commences with the wind West and thick fog. The Schooner Daring *came to the Island this morning before daylight and the superintendent came on shore. We landed the provisions for the Island, and also Mr. Nesbitt with his family and things who has come to the Island to take charge of the Eastern Establishment. We shipped on board the vessel two horses with six barrels of hides, a lot of old iron, a lot of yellow metal, three barrels of seal oil, a pair of cart wheels to be repaired, and Charles Adams' things, and at half past seven PM the vessel sailed for Halifax. This day ends with the wind West and thick fog with rain.*

The East End post had been vacant since before Christmas of the previous year, when Charles Adams departed because of his sudden illness. From this entry it seems Adams would not be returning to Sable Island, as his replacement Mr. Nesbitt settled in with his own family.

It took a few days to acclimatise Nesbitt to the new post, providing him with provisions and supplies to run his station, a wooden cart, and bringing him horses. Nesbitt and another man had a great deal of trouble trying to drive down a cow and a calf to the East End, as the cow would not be driven away from the rest of the herd. It took a few attempts over several days to coax the animal to its new home.

On July 27th, a ship was spotted on shore, and the men leapt into action.

Monday, July 27th

Commences with the wind East, a strong breeze and dark weather, but no fog. At 4 1/2 AM the man that had the look out saw from the flag staff a ship and shore on the South Side near the West End, in the spot where the Myrtle *and* Glasgow *were lost. We immediately got in a team of horses, got the life boat hauled into the lake with another boat. I sent a hand up the North*

Side with a team to meet us at the wreck, and I was proceeding up the lake with the boats when it came on to rain very heavy and blow a strong gale. The wind being about three paints across the land where the ship was, I observed her cant, head off, and I could plainly perceive that she was working off, and at about half past five or six o'clock in the morning she went off and was soon out of sight. I had hoisted the colours before we left the house to show them that we saw them, and we were about halfway to her when she got off. At this time it was blowing hard and raining hard. I landed on the South Side and sent two hands up the beach but they returned without seeing any thing more of her, and we returned home with a good soaking in the rain. We had to leave one boat and haul the other down with the horses, it blowed so hard. In the afternoon, I sent a man on horseback round the West End but could see nothing new about the beach. This day ends with the wind ENE, with heavy rain and thick weather.

Here, a note is scribbled in the margin, reading:

Note: I gave Martin Clye, John Stevens, John H. Darby, and James Darby, certificates for one wreck in 1842 and one in 1843, and I gave Charles Adams a certificate for one wreck in 1843, which is the only one he was entitled to. The certificate is dated July 19th, 1846.

Darby doesn't mention the name of the almost-wrecked ship, but thankfully it departed without any lives being lost.

In August, misadventures came one after another. One of the best cows on the island was injured by a bull and had her hips out of place. They nursed the cow for three weeks, until they decided she didn't stand a chance to get better. "She had got hurt some way by the bulls," Darby later wrote, "and when we opened her, we found both her hip bones out of place, and a large piece broke off one of them, and all very much swelled bruised and mortified. This was the healthiest cow on the Island for raising calves, and never lost one with sickness." Nesbitt also turned up at the main station, his cart having broken for the second time since arriving on the island. "He cannot repair it himself," Darby wrote. "I had to send my son and another hand with him. They had to take it all to pieces and straighten the iron arms of the axle." A few days later, the crumbling pig pen was torn down to be rebuilt. Timber was hauled up to build a new one with an entirely new foundation. It took them several weeks to construct.

Around this time, the *Lady Echo* was sailing around Sable Island, with Captain Kimball and crew on board. They were participating in the mackerel hunt, and occasionally landed on shore for provisions. Darby lent him a net on shares, but nothing was caught. The *Victoria*, with Captain Crowell, was also fishing the waters, and not catching much. He came ashore for barrels of water, and by the end of August both he and Kimball were reporting the fish were very plentiful.

On the 6th of September, however, the weather took a turn, and in the morning fog Stevens came up from the North Side of the island. He reported that there was a ship on shore near his house, and all hands rushed into action. The horses and carts were taken out and brought to meet the ship. Rescuing shipwrecked crews was a very manual task, with little technology to help. Boats, ropes, hooks, and lanterns were the tools of the trade. This stranded ship was the *Detroit*, and fortunately the crew had managed to get on shore in their own boats, along with some of their baggage. There were twelve men in total, including Captain Lowell, plus the captain's wife among them.

The sea was heavy in the morning, but became smoother in the afternoon. As the ship hadn't started taking on water, Darby believed they might be able to get her afloat again. He took a stream anchor and cable out for them to try and heave the ship off, but she would not move. The anchor was too light, and it wouldn't hold in the soft sand that surrounded the beach. The *Detroit* sat there, stuck but upright in the sand.

The crew of the ship slept on the beach that night, while the captain, his wife, and the mate slept at Darby's house. Their baggage was hauled into one of the empty buildings that served as a warehouse for shipwrecked goods.

At high tide the following morning, they again tried to dislodge the stuck ship. "The ship tight and sallying about quite lively at high water," Darby wrote, "but as this anchor would not hold and there was no boat fit to carry out a bower anchor, I made a raft on four 80 gallon casks on which we took the small bower anchor, about 15 cwt and 60 or 70 fathoms of good manila hawser, 80 inch, and laid it down outside the inner bar. We hove tight and all hands remained by the ship until after high water, about 10 o'clock at night, and hove her off several fathoms." There was a fair prospect of getting her off, Darby decided, the sea being smooth, and so the crew slept on the beach another night.

At high water on the second morning, they hoisted both topsails and topgallant sails, hove on the hawser, and moved the ship astern about 50 or 60 yards. The tide suddenly left them, but Darby decided there was a fair prospect of them getting off on the night tide. "I arranged with the Master that he was to pay the Establishment a hundred dollars for what assistance he had received and might receive if the ship got off, and before night the people got their baggage on board again. I had two carts loaded with the Captain's baggage standing on the bank ready to shove on board if she got afloat, had our boat on the beach already all the time, and was oft in her every night alongside the ship, but at 7 PM the wind hauled to the NW and the tide rose. The sea hove in, and she rather forged a little, dragging that heavy anchor with her. The tide fell and we left her quite tight and nothing injured." The mate and rest of the crew stayed on board the ship that night, and the captain and his wife stayed at Darby's house for another night. Hard rain squalls hit that night, bringing thunder and lightning.

On the third morning, Darby and the captain returned to the ship. At high water, the sea had broken all over her, and she hove around broadside to the beach. "I waited until the tide fell a little and got a man on board to see if she made any water, but she did not as far as we could ascertain at the time, and the captain not yet willing to abandon her, and I knowing we could do nothing with her now, I went with all our people up home to work at the hay, only leaving my son with the captain to assist him in anything he wished to do." There was only so much time that Darby could dedicate to waiting for this ship to move, since the lives of its crew were not in danger, and winter was coming. There were too many chores to hold their attention.

That evening, Darby spotted the Schooner *Victoria* and Captain Crowell laying off the island. He made a signal to him, and Crowell came on shore. "He informed me he was going to Halifax, having wet all his salt, and I gave him a letter to the Commissioners at Halifax." Captain Lowell was still not willing to abandon his stranded ship, and did not take the opportunity to return his crew to Halifax by way of the other vessel.

On September 10th, Darby wrote that they heard nothing from the stuck ship all day, and that all the hands were very much fatigued from their efforts over the past week. They got some hay stacked, but could do little else. Darby's son came up from the ship to say that Captain Lowell had given up all hopes of getting the ship off, as she had taken on a great deal of water. He asked for as much help as he could get, and Darby sent down two hands with a team immediately. "After dinner I went down with all hands and another team and commenced stripping the ship. We hauled her sails, blocks, and running rigging with the baggage and provisions all to the warehouse over a road of two miles, and hauled the chains, anchors, boats, and standing rigging into the safest place we could find on the North Beach."

The next three days were spent carting things from the ship to the warehouse. The cargo was all moved the first day, then the ship was dismantled. Leaden lumps, windlass iron, and everything else of value went into the storage rooms. Darby took an inventory of all that had been collected with Captain Lowell to ensure that the ship's items were not mixed up with the island's possessions.

On September 15th, the crew, captain, and his wife brought their luggage to the main station to set up in accommodations until they could be transported to the mainland. In the afternoon, Darby spied Captain Kimball laying off the landing, fishing for mackerel. The weather was moderate and dark that day, and after everyone had gone to bed, Darby was woken by a knock at the door near 11 o'clock. He met Captain Kimball, who informed him that a sudden gust of wind and a heavy squall from the North had thrown his vessel on shore. "I struck a light, got a lantern and went with all hands to the North Beach," he wrote later. "It was blowing very hard in squalls and the sea breaking already all round the vessel, which was quite close in to the shore. We got the people landed, all wet. We got them to the house, made a good fire, and prepared a bed for them as well as I could, and I went to bed again." There were 8 men in Captain Kimball's crew, now added to the number of extra persons to feed and house on the island.

They worked to remove the cargo from the wrecked *Lady Echo* the following day. She was high on the beach and half full of water in the morning, and they managed to get out 158 barrels of mackerel, 8 barrels of salt, and 16 empty barrels. Her sails, rigging cables, and anchors were brought on shore. At 3 PM, the Schooner *Daring* hove in sight, coming to the island. Darby attempted to take a boat over to board, but the sea was too dangerous and he returned to carrying supplies from the *Lady Echo*.

The rest of the entry for September 16th and the entries for the 17th, 18th, and first half of the 19th are lost from Darby's journals. They no doubt detailed the extensive deconstruction of the two wrecked ships, and included Captain Kimball's return to Halifax from the island aboard the *Daring*. On the 19th, the people of the island witnessed the wreck of the *Arno*, which is mostly preserved. Darby spoke about this storm and wreck in greater lengths at a public lecture many years later, the transcript of which is in Chapter 5.

> *Saturday, September 19th*
> *(Continued) the Island, after digging a road through the North Ridge to the beach. The gale had blown down our fences, unroofed two buildings and blown the shingles off other buildings. I had two spare hands to put up the fences round the gardens to keep the hogs and cattle from destroying them. At 4 1/2 PM, a vessel hove into sight off the North Side and we soon discovered that she was running down before the wind for the Island, and at this time the sea was breaking mountains high one mile and a half off from the land. She was a Schooner under a close roofed mainsail and jib. At 5 1/2 PM, she had come through all the*

breakers on to the dry beach, and we got the people, eight men, on shore from off the jib boom end. We took them to the house, gave them some refreshment, made them a bed by a good fire for the night. She proved to be fishermen from Banquereau bound home. She belonged to Plymouth N.S. and left the bank with the first of the gale. They had some of their sails blown away, and during the most violent part of the gale, had to send under beme poles, which brought them down on the Island. They first anchored just in sight of land in 20 fathoms of water, where after laying some time they concluded to cut their cables and run the vessel on shore before night. This ends with the wind North a strong gale, but clear weather.

It was miraculous that nobody was injured in the wreck of the *Arno*. The storm had been fierce, and the ship had been launched headfirst into the island. They spent the next few days stripping and hauling materials from the *Arno* into the storage buildings. Captain Crowell of the *Victoria* stopped by to see how everyone fared in the gale, reporting that it had been very violent at sea. He had been moored off the West head, but the storm had parted his chain cable, lost an anchor, and drifted him out to sea. His windlass had also been injured, and the people on the island did some light smith work to repair it for him.

Nesbitt returned from the East End, his cart broken yet again. Darby and the others did the best they could to fix it. "I am afraid it won't stand long," he remarked in his entry for September 23rd, "and the man cannot live where he is without a cart to collect his fuel or haul home his provisions." Besides the perpetual broken cart, Nesbitt seemed to have adjusted well to his duties at the East End. Darby rarely mentioned him in his journal, which could be considered a good thing.

On September 24th, the men were busy hauling salt out of the *Arno* when another ship came into sight. It was the Schooner *Union*, sailed by Captain Kimball from Halifax on his way to collect the materials and cargo from the *Lady Echo*. In a few days, they managed to load it all plus that of the *Arno*, the Captain, his crew, and their baggage and stores.

With all their shipwrecked visitors gone from the island, the workers set about repairing their own damages from the storm. The gale had blown shingles off the provision store, and the shingles and roof of the capstan house needed repair. The working boat was repaired, but they had nothing on hand with which they could make new oars. They washed out the house where the two crews had been living, mended hay stacks, repaired doors, and laid new doorsteps.

The rest of the month and days following were spent gathering more cargo and materials from the wrecks as the sea broke them up. After so much time spent in the ocean, one man from the island was laid up with salt water boils. It was inevitable that the people involved in these intense rescues would suffer various physical repercussions from their labours. Darby gave the others a day off to repair their shoes and other clothing, "that always gets very much destroyed in working so much in the water."

With three shipwrecks in a row, the islanders were overworked and exhausted from both the physical labour and the stress. It was fortunate that no lives were lost in the wrecks of the *Detroit*, the *Lady Echo*, or the *Arno*. The sea and weather was unpredictable, and months often passed with no wrecks at all. Storms peaked in the autumn during hurricane season, the severity of which is still familiar to maritimers today. It was imperative that Darby and the people of the establishment were prepared at all times for the unexpected.

Chapter Four

Shifting Powers

In April of the year 1847, a man named Robert Nichols was hired to work on Sable Island. His tenure on the island was brief; by the end of November he was sent back to the mainland, having abandoned his post after constant disagreements with Joseph Darby. These events instigated the final investigation of Darby's activities on the island, concluding with a series of charges laid against him that saw the instalment of both a new superintendent and a new board in place of the commissioners.

The only journals surviving from the year 1847 are from October 1st, the day after Nichols disappeared from his work. No records remain of Darby's account of the summer in which Nichols was employed – whether it was lost intentionally, or in the accident post-World War Two, we can't say. However, later testimonies provided in 1848 do fill in some of these gaps.

Most noteworthy from the single 1847 journal is Darby's summary at the end of the year. It outlines his grievances with the island and its management, highlighting the tense relationship between the commissioners, some of the hired men, and himself. "Thus ends the year 1847," Darby wrote, "and to me it has been a year of misery and unhappiness, which I attribute wholly to the misguided policy of the

Commissioners. Two men has given notice to leave the Island as soon as their times are up in March and April, and I expect that two other men will leave when their time is up sometime in May and June. The perilous and fatiguing labour that was performed saving the *Levant's* materials, I fancy, will long be remembered by those that worked at it, and they will, some of them, not run the risk of meeting such another job for the same remuneration. J Darby."

To piece together the story of Darby and Nichols' conflict, we begin with what Darby wrote just after the man disappeared from his post. On October 1st, Darby remarked that all the hands were away working in the morning except for Nichols. "Nichols is not to be found anywhere," he commented among the details of the day's labours. "No sign of Nichols," the next day, too. "In the afternoon Stevens came up, I gave him one gallon of liquor, some lumbers, and gave large pigs to keep over the winter. He has seen nothing of Nichols, and I begin to think that he has got on board of some of the vessels and gone off, as he said he would not work on the island for a hundred pounds a month." Darby alluded to a disagreement that took place previously.

On October 4th, Nichols was finally discovered. "Stevens came up this morning and brought up Nichols' horse," Darby wrote, "and he says that Nesbitt brought him to his house yesterday evening, and that he has been at the East End house, and now as he will not conform to the rules of the Establishment, I will have no more to do with him, but will send him off the first opportunity, and as he is idle I will give him bread and meat, and he may cook for himself, and he has already shown himself a notorious liar by saying that I struck him." Darby's frustration comes through clearly. There were specific rules established for rations given to working men, idle men, and women and children on the island. Nichols was given bread and meat, and freedom to cook — this meant access to basic cooking resources like flour and salt from the stores. There were plenty of places for Nichols to prepare food for himself, as there were small makeshift kitchens for castaway people at all the stations. Darby recorded fixing up one such place on November 1st out of an old camboose, a cooking space from the galley of a ship, with a little house over it for shelter.

Finally, on November 18th, the *Daring* arrived at sunrise. After getting on board and landing supplies, they shipped around two tons of rod steel, seven tons of new iron, and 300 lbs of new sheet copper along with the camboose from the *Levant*. "Robert Nichols went off in this vessel," Darby wrote, "and I sent his things to the Commissioners." The ship set sail that night, and Darby likely hoped that was the last he was to hear of Nichols.

The rest of November passed without incident. On the first of December, everyone moved into their winter quarters as the weather became wetter and colder. They hauled out compost heaps, cleaned out the privies and dug pits to bury the contents, and caulked the plank walls of the buildings to keep them warm. Darby spotted another unique sight on December 12th: "at 9 AM this morning I saw a bright star bearing South about 45 degrees above the horizon. The sun was about an hour and a half high with a thin haze round her, but overhead was very clear, and the star shone quite bright but in the course of another hour the sun got up out of the haze and we lost sight of the star." Beyond this, life went on for the people of Sable Island as they prepared for another harsh winter.

Meanwhile, Robert Nichols was back in Halifax and brewing with dissatisfaction over his treatment on Sable Island. He took his grievances to the office of the commissioners, where he sat down and provided a lengthy account of his interactions with Joseph Darby. They were eager to hear all he had to say. The commissioners were unhappy with Darby's lack of obedience, and Nichols' serious claims were the opportunity they needed to investigate Darby further.

A letter was written to the Lieutenant Governor, Sir John Harvey. Prior to becoming the lieutenant governor of Nova Scotia in 1846, Harvey had enjoyed a long military career and was the lieutenant governor for Prince Edward Island, New Brunswick, and then Civil Governor of Newfoundland. In these roles he managed to settle a relative peace over provincial political turmoil, and he approached Nova Scotia with the intention of doing the same. However, in 1846 Nova Scotia already had two fairly well established political parties, and Harvey was not able to do as he wished. His attempts to convince the Liberals (known as Reformers) and Conservatives of Nova Scotia to join together in a coalition government were unsuccessful.

The failure of a coalition government meant that an election was imminent. Though Harvey still hoped to unite the two parties, an announcement came from the colonial secretary, Earl Grey. Grey declared that it was now up to provinces to govern themselves with their own parties. This declaration put an end to Harvey's prospects of success and forced him to work within the new electoral system.

The Liberal party won the election, and became the first party-based administration in pre-Confederation Canada. Joseph Howe and the party's Executive Council were responsible for much of the campaigning for this significant victory, and in February 1848, the their leader James Boyle Uniacke was put in place as the Premier, though that exact title was not much in use yet. Nova Scotia was launching in a new direction, and one that John Harvey was begrudgingly forced to accept. Harvey was friends with Joseph Howe, who became the provincial secretary, and both men worked to advance the progress of the provincial government.

It was during all this tumult that the commissioners of Sable Island decided to involve Harvey in their case against Darby. They sent a letter to Harvey detailing their concerns, and a copy of this was sent to Darby as well. On the 2nd of March, 1848, Darby wrote to the commissioners in reply to this letter.

> *Sable Island, March 2nd, 1848*
> *Gentlemen,*
> *On reperusing the copy of your letter, no date, to His Excellency, I find that you have made some statements that are not strictly true, besides many insinuations injurious to character. I hope you will not take it amiss if I caution you against, and I will make a few remarks on some of the most pointed, and first you had listed that I knew before I came here what was to be done; I knew not of boats and carts to be made at my expense, all the rest I knew very well. You have said that I have done no more than any good man would have done. You do well to introduce the word (good). I have indeed done all that I could, which is what very*

few good men could or would have done, and particularly either one of the men that are my accusers. You have said that my family has been supported at the public expense. That is not correct, my family has on a great measure supported this Establishment, and made it what it is by their hard labour, and if every servant of the government had laboured as hard to benefit the government as me and my family has done, the government would have been better off, and the servants less expense. And but for the great labours of my family here, I think that the Establishment would yet have been in the same disgraceful state that it was in when I came to it. You are not aware of my having laid out money for materials for building boats, that has not been refunded to me, yet I have done it, and some of the boats are here yet to be sold (also money advanced to the servants, to enable them to do their duty). Most of the money has not been refunded, and it is a pity for your own sake that you would confess to be so ignorant. You say that in 1832 I applied to you for extra remuneration for this extra service, and to show the world that you admitted the claim to be just, you say that you increased my salary 23 percent. That is right, but supposing I had left the island in 1842, how could that have remunerated me, besides I had not fallen out with my salary, although it was tolerable for the duties of the superintendent, yet it was not enough to cover the salaries of a Cartwright and a boat builder too. You have stated to His Excellency that within the present year or past year you were called upon to reprimand me for practices on my part that were injurious to the respectability and interests of the Establishment. I have practiced nothing against the respectability or interests of the Establishment, without it is working too hard, and making too much money for it, that is injurious, so my great and Herculean labours for the past year fully shows. And every thing that I have done has.a contrary effort from being injurious, and all the injury that has been done to the Establishment has been done by others, and not by me. The next thing I have to notice is where you state that you have endeavoured to meet my views in every way that you can. Pardon me gentlemen if I plainly tell you this is not so. Have you met with my views with regard to liquor, have you met my views with regards to provisions, have you met my views with regard to extra remuneration to the people? No, your views are diametrically opposed to mine and all the trouble that I have here with the people is the result of it. I am yet able to do a great deal for this Establishment, and I much desire to be permitted to do it in peace.

And remain your obedient servant,
Joseph Darby
To the commissioners for the affairs of Sable Island at Halifax, NS

In addition to sending this letter to the commissioners, Darby also wrote to John Harvey to clear his name. This did not sit well with the commissioners. Darby's defence made them look very bad, and as the commissioners were also men that held other positions of influence in Halifax, they would not be keen for any stain on their reputations. At the end of March, they wrote to the office of the lieutenant governor again.

Halifax, March 29th, 1848
Sir,
We have learned by a letter lately received from Mr Joseph Darby, Superintendent at Sable Island, that he has made a communication to His Excellency the Lieut. Governor in reply to the report which we had the honour to make his Excellency on the 6th December last, and which received His Excellency's approbation.

We beg to ask the favour of you to assure His Excellency that we are prepared to substantiate if necessary all the parts stated in that report. And we would not now intrude on His Excellency's time, but that the tone of all Darby's communications has lately been so inconsistent with propriety that we consider it necessary to bring his conduct under the notice of the Government.

We have before stated to His Excellency that as Mr Darby had with some exceptions conducted himself to the satisfaction of the commissioners, we were inclined to pave over rather severe charges, hoping that the severe reprimands, which we have on those occasions felt it to be our duty to give him, would have operated beneficially on his future conduct.

We lament to inform His Excellency that the forbearance on the part of the commissioners has not resulted in the good consequences we had hoped for, and we are now compelled to repeat that from information lately received with reference to his treatment of some of the passengers of the American Schooner "Fulton", lately wrecked on Sable Island, and his general conduct of late, both as regards Nichols and other, it is necessary to have a serious investigation into the charges alleged against him.

We have the honor therefore respectfully to request that His Excellency will be pleased to order, if it shall appear necessary to him, that Mr. Joseph Darby shall proceed to Halifax at the first favourable opportunity for the purpose of answering to the charges lately made against him, which if substantiated would in our opinion operate unfavourably on the hitherto good character of the Humane Establishment at Sable Island.

We have the honor to be, Sir, your most obt humble servants
E Wallace
E Cunard
LP Miller
Commissioners of Sable Island

The commissioners needed to convince the lieutenant governor that they had done everything possible to improve the situation on Sable Island, but that Darby had made it impossible. They concluded that the solution to this was to bring Darby to Halifax, where he would be unable to escape from his charges by means of well-written letters.

One of the charges that they were levying against Darby was that he was using his position of advantage to manipulate the Halifax auctions on shipwrecks from Sable to his own benefit. These noisy, damp auctions took place in the shipyards of Halifax, where warehouses stored the wrecked goods and merchants and investors alike gathered to try and get a deal. It wasn't uncommon for agents of wealthy people to bid on lots on their behalf, and so tracing the ownership of certain purchases became easily muddled. There was one particular shipwreck that was the main subject of this accusation: the *Fulton*, a ship that was bought by a man named John Campbell. Campbell was only interested in certain parts of the auction lot, and subsequently sold the rest to John Darby, Joseph Darby's son. The commissioners took this as a conflict of interest, and were refusing to release the lot to John Campbell.

Suddenly mixed up in this case, Campbell wrote a letter to the lieutenant governor to clear himself of any suspicions of foul play.

> *Halifax, 4th April 1848*
> *To His Excellency Lieutenant General John Harvey R.C.B.*
> *May it please Your Excellency,*
> *It having been notified to me, that some doubts have been thrown upon the correctness of a purchase made by me for a recent sale under the order of the commissioners of Sable Island of the schooner Fulton wrecked at the Isle of Sable. I beg leave to submit for the consideration of Your Excellency a plain statement of the facts, so far as I was concerned in the transactions and in order to place the validity and in order to place the validity of my statements beyond a doubt I have determined to verify those statements on both. Having noticed in the public papers that a sale of wrecked materials and a vessel were to be sold at auction. I attended the sale, being myself engaged in shipping, in the hope that I might obtain articles which I might find useful at a cheap rate. There was a large concourse of persons present and although I bid on several of the lots of the materials, yet I did not become the purchaser of any of them, but on the vessel being put up. I with many others bid for her and although I believe the wreck was at first set up for one pound, yet eventually it was knocked down to me at the sum of twenty five pounds, the persons who bid on the wreck I cannot remember but I think the Gentleman who proceeded my last bid was the pawn. I beg distinctly to state that I made the purchase bona fide from the information I received,*

through the public prints and from the statement made publicly at the sale in reference to the state of the vessel and her cargo, which I understood consisted of pickled fish and dry fish, and some copper. I subsequently sold a part of the vessel to a Mr John Darby, for whom I intended to intrust the more active duties in attending to the wreck and cargo. I had not previously known Mr. Darby, and made the purchase without exchanging any conversation with him or without any compact or understanding either with Mr Darby or any other persons whatever. I consider the transaction one of purely a public nature and beg distinctly to state that in the whole transaction I have acted with perfect fairness and uprightness, and I trust no impediments will be used to prevent me from reaping any benefits which might result to me from a purchase made in such a public manner.

I have the honor to be, Your Excellency, most obedient humble servant
John Campbell

In response to this letter, the lieutenant governor's office turned to the commissioners with frustration. Neither John Harvey or Joseph Howe were interested in being the middleman in this conflict; they had bigger problems to worry about. In order to settle the matter, it was decided that William Townsend, a reliable merchant and politician from Yarmouth, would visit Sable Island for a proper investigation. Joseph Howe informed the commissioners of this by a letter where he interestingly refers to Darby as the governor of Sable Island. An understandable mistake, as this was essentially the function that Darby served on the island, but it was a distinction that greatly annoyed the commissioners. To them, Darby was nothing but a wayward employee.

Provincial Secretary's Office
Halifax, April 7th 1858
   Gentlemen,
      It appears to His Excellency the Lieutenant Governor that John Campbell Esquire and not Mr John Darby as stated in the

draft of your letter to the Governor of the Isle of Sable was the purchaser of the Fulton. *I am instructed to authorize you to hand over the property purchased and afford to Mr Campbell the usual facilities for its remuneration.*

I am also commanded to inform you that His Excellency the Lieutenant Governor has appointed Mr William Townsend to proceed to Sable Island to investigate the complaints professed by you against the Governor of the Island and to report generally upon the state of the Humane Establishment there.

Signed Joseph Howe

On this same day, Joseph Howe wrote to Townsend to inform him of his orders.

Provincial Secretary's Office
Halifax, 7th April 1848
Sir,
His Excellency the Lieutenant Governor, having been pleased to appoint you a commission to enquire, generally, into the state of the Public Establishment on Sable Island and the condition and value of any wrecked property on the Island, particularly the wreck of the Fulton. *I beg to endorse your commission and instruction — and have to request that you will proceed in the execution of this task without any unnecessary delay.*
I am, Sir, your obedient servant,
Joseph Howe
Mr William Townshend

An official statement followed from the lieutenant governor's office, with additional details about his orders.

By His Excellency Lieutenant-General Sir John Harvey, Knight Commander of the Most Honourable Military Order of the Bath, Knight Commander of the Royal Hanoverian Guelphic Order, Lieutenant-Governor and Commander in Chief, in and over Her Majesty's Province of Nova Scotia and its Dependencies, &c. &c. &c.

To Mr. William Townsend,
By virtue of the power and authority in me vested by Law, I do by there presents constitute and appoint you to be a commissioner duly authorized to proceed to the Isle of Sable in the said Province, and to inquire into and make due report to me upon the condition, position, and value of the wreck of the Fulton. Also into the situation and circumstances of William Williams, a minor hiring on the island, whom if you shall deem it expedient or necessary you are authorized with his own consent to bring to Halifax. Also you are to enquire into the condition of one William Etter on the said island and by whose authority and when he was there placed, and is now detained, and whether at any time or times and when other and what persons are on have been there detained and by whose authority and for what causes. And generally you are required to report upon the state of the Public Establishment on and the management of the Island and to make all necessary inquires for this purpose. And to take all lawful measures requisite in the premises.
Given under my hand and seal at Halifax this seventh day of April in the eleventh year of HM reign AD 1848.
By His Excellency's Command
Joseph Howe

This letter references another concern of the commissioners: that there were two people on the island unlawfully. Nichols gave them this lead in his testimony. Nichols stated that there was a minor hired on the island named William Williams, and that there was a man being confined there against his will named William Etter. These concerning statements were chief among the topics for investigation by Townsend, and rightfully so.

The commissioners were immediately suspicious of the in-person investigation. They had recommended bringing Darby to Halifax;

they never intended for someone to visit the island, where they might interview more people. If the investigator was not aligned with their purposes, it was possible that the crown would disapprove of what they saw happening on Sable Island and take Darby's side in the matter, blaming the commissioners for all the problems Darby had tried to fix without their support. Taking this investigation as a slight against themselves, they protested against sending Townsend to Sable, and repeated their insistence in bringing Darby to Halifax. The final line of the following letter made it clear that they took this quite personally.

> Halifax, 8th April 1848
> Joseph Howe, Provincial Secretary
> Sir,
> We have to acknowledge your communication under date of the 7th April and in reply beg respectfully to submit for the information of His Excellency the Lieut. Governor the following facts relative to the sale purchase of the "Fulton". The vessel was put up in the presence of the American consul who was acting as agent and on behalf of the owners, as well as a large assembly of private individuals, and was sold to Mr John Campbell for £25. The state and position of the schooner being as fully described as the information we had at the time enabled us to do. Subsequently we received the Provincial Secretary's intersections conveying to us the Lieut. Governor's directions to retain possession of the vessel until further investigation should be made, which we complied with. And have now in light of the instruction conveyed to us in your letter of yesterday given an order to the Superintendent of Sable Island to hand over the same to Mr. Campbell.
> We cannot refrain from remarking that His Excellency should have been advised to appoint Mr. William Townsend to proceed to Sable Island to investigate the complaints made by us against the Superintendent of the island where no specific charges have been proffered against him by the Commissioners to the Lieut. Governor. Best as complaints were laid to the charge of the Superintendent of Sable Island, the commissioners deemed it

their duty to address an official letter to the Provincial Secretary respectfully soliciting His Excellency to direct the Superintendent of the Island to proceed to Halifax to explain or refute the accusation alleged against him, to which communication the Commissioners received no reply.

They further consider themselves found to state for the information of the Lieutenant Governor, that with all due deference they conceive that all matters and charges against the Superintendent of the Island or the Commissioners could be more satisfactorily investigated here than by the appointment of a single individual to proceed to the Island. Should the appointment of Mr. Townsend be made with the intention of an enquiry into any matter which may involve the Commissioners, or should any charges have been preferred against them, they respectfully solicit His Excellency the Lieut. Governor would be pleased to direct the copies of the same to be transmitted to them, in order that they may vindicate their character from any imputations cast upon them.

We have the honor to be, Sir, your most humble servants
W Wallace
E Cunard
EP Miller
Commissioners of Sable Island

Joseph Howe replied to this shortly after. He told the commissioners that Townsend would still be going to the island regardless of their request, and that if they wished, they could come down themselves to look over the orders detailing what he was going to investigate. He clearly had no time for their scheming. A few days later, a sheepish reply from the commissioners followed.

Halifax, 11 April 1848
Sir,
We have the honor to acknowledge the receipt of your note of the 10th last, informing us by command of His Excellency the

> *Lieut. Governor that Mr Townsend's instructions on his mission to Sable Island be at the Provincial Secretary's office and are open to our perusal. We beg lease to observe with deference to our communication of the 8th last that we did not presume to seek for the documents you allude to, as his Excellency the Lieut. Governor did not think proper to communicate them to us previous to the departure of Mr Townsend. Such a request on our part to be highly improper, and wanting in the respect due to His Excellency.*
>
> *We would take the liberty of observing that the principal object of our communication was to pray His Excellency to afford us copies of any letters or other documents if any such were in possession of the Government reflecting either on the conduct of the Superintendent or ourselves, in order that we might have had an opportunity afforded us by obtaining the necessary evidence to refute the same.*
>
> *We have the honor to be, Sir, your humble servants*
> *W Wallace*
> *E Cunard*
> *GP Miller*
> *Commissioners of Sable Island*

Following these communications, Townsend departed for his investigation on Sable Island. As Darby's journals from this time have been lost, there are no accounts of his time spent there from the perspective of the islanders outside of this report and the letters that followed. From what we know of Darby, he likely saw this visit as both a terrible nuisance and a wonderful opportunity. His daily tasks would be interrupted and his leadership would be questioned, but he finally had the ear of someone other than the commissioners who could bring about change. He would have been keen to show Townsend the many projects he had started of his own initiative, and the ways in which the commissioners tried to foil his attempts at improving the establishment.

Townsend spent five days on Sable Island with Joseph Darby. He was welcomed by the superintendent and shown around, and spent a great deal of time pouring over the map that Darby made of the island.

Darby could not spare all of his time to escort Townsend, however, which left the investigator to walk around the establishment and the island by himself. He interviewed the labourers, took detailed notes on the state of affairs, and carefully scrutinised the dynamics at play on the island.

He returned to Halifax with a great deal of information, and put together a lengthy report for Joseph Howe. Beyond its role as an important document in the conflict between Darby and the commissioners, Townsend's report provides an extensive and critical view of Sable Island as it stood in the mid-1840s from the perspective of a neutral party.

Halifax, 26th April 1848
Sir,
Having received the commission entrusted to my care dated April 7th on the 8th, I proceeded to Sable Island on the same day by the opportunity pointed out in your letter.

I arrived there in the morning of the 11th and left on the morning of the 15th, arriving here again on the afternoon of the 18th.

On reaching the Island, I presented my commission to the Superintendent and it is due to him to state that I received from him all the assistance I required with the greatest courtesy.

I immediately commenced the duties assigned me by the said commission and by leave to hand you the surveyed report thereof.

I have the honor to be, Sir, your most obed. Servant
William Townsend
The Honorable Joseph Howe
Provincial Secretary

<u>*Report*</u>

As the commission directs me to report generally on the state of Sable Island, it may not be out of place before taking up the specified objects to note a few facts touching the founding and intention of the Establishment. Also the production and resources of the Island.

To do so, it will be proper to state that the Island is at present about twenty five miles long and about two miles broad, composed entirely of sand, very uneven, and varying in height from ten to one hundred feet, the highest part being towards the East End. From ten to twelve miles of the West End have been washed away within the last thirty years.

There is a salt water lake on the Island about fourteen miles long and on an average about one mile wide, with an outlet to the ocean at present on the North Side.

On the north side of the lake the Island is high, on the south side it is best little more than a beach that divides it from the ocean.

The first fixed establishment on the Island by this province was founded in the year one thousand eight hundred and three at the recommendation of the late Sir John Wentworth, then Governor, and for the humane purpose of affording assistance and relief to all persons when accident might cast before its shores.

It is now supplied with all the means for effecting the objects intended, having accommodation to shelter, if necessity required, about five hundred persons, or even more. An excellent life and other suitable boats, and a stock of provisions is kept on hand sufficient with live stock, to meet almost any emergency as regards food, with the exception of bread stuffs.

The only natural productions of the Island are a species of rank grass, mixed with a kind of wild pea, and which covers a large portion of the Island. Cranberries grow in abundance and some blueberries, also strawberries of good flavour and large size. There is not a tree nor a bush of any size on the Island, and the only source for fuel is drift wood, stranded timber cargoes and the hulls of wrecked vessels.

The grass mentioned above is excellent food for the cattle as grass, but makes poor feed as hay, and were it not for the light mixture of the wild pea, the domestic horses would scarcely touch it. The cattle cannot be worked on it alone, and during the winter months there is much for them to do, especially should there be any wrecks.

There are roaming at large, as near as can be estimated,

about two hundred and fifty horses and the number is increasing. Since the present superintendent has been residing on the Island, now about eighteen years, there has been about three hundred shipped off the Island, and I think he informed me that there was not more than seventy when he went there. In severe winters numbers die, but few died the last winter.

There are a large number of rabbits on the Island which are excellent fresh food, and were it not for the destruction of the young ones by the rats, which are very numerous, they would increase fast and form a good reserve in case of scarcity. In addition to their allowance of salt meat, transient persons are allowed to use them twice a week, but in general they use them oftener.

The lake and the shores of the Island abound with seals, and sufficient oil is made for the use of the Island and to spare. Nine I am of opinion might be taken in the winter or early spring and made into oil for the benefit of the Establishment.

The cod and mackerel fisheries in the vicinity of the Island are excellent, especially the mackerel fishing in the fall, and which might be pursued to advantage. Enough were taken and cured last season for the use of the Establishment and some to spare. They are generally of the finest quality.

A quantity of blackfish were thrown on the shores of the Island last winter which have been made into oil and it is now ready to come off, as will be seen by the memorandum of articles ready for shipment. I am of the opinion that the above description of fish being thrown upon its shores is not a singular case.

As game, there is an abundance of ducks, and also pigeons and plovers in their season.

There are on the Island, of domestic animals, twenty horses, forty three head of horned cattle, three sheep, about twenty pigs, and a good stock of poultry. The whole divided as will be seen in the schedule of moveable property, all of which, except the sheep, belong to the Establishment.

The superintendent informed me that there was a great difficulty in bringing calves over their first year in consequence of disease which is principally an effusion of the gall. If stock of this kind could be large increased, it would form a profitable item for the Establishment, as the horned cattle that are not worked do much better on the Island hay than the domestic horses.

The raising of sheep, up to this time, has been almost a total failure. This is much to be regretted as a good stock of sheep would be a valuable resource to the Island, which with an increasing stock of horned cattle, might supply itself with meat.

Sufficient butter is made on the Island for use of the Establishment, and last season there was cured at the principal station about twenty hundred weights of pork and the same quantity of beef, and a small quantity at the other stations.

With the assistance of stable manure and bog mud, a sufficient supply of potatoes and garden vegetables is generally raised for the ordinary supply of the Establishment. The superintendent informed me that last year they dug four hundred buckets of potatoes, partially touched with disease but better than the previous year, but the garden crop last year was almost totally destroyed by the rats.

There are two subjects at least that for the benefit of the Island should have much care bestowed on them, and they are the raising of sheep, and destroying of rats.

Oats are sown in limited quantity but do not come to perfection and are generally cut for fodder.

To keep the cattle up from midwinter to the time of the grass growing in spring, it is necessary to send oats from Halifax, as the working cattle — horses especially — could not be worked to any extent without extra feed.

Presuming that the danger to navigation that extends from the Island and the position of the Island itself are too well known to need mention in this report, I have passed over any description of them.

What at present may be called the Establishment of Sable Island, consists of four stations — three inhabited and one uninhabited — as will be hereafter explained — with a superintendent and nine other persons in charge of the whole, who with their families and William Etter make up twenty seven persons in all resident of the Island at this time, and divided as hereafter will be seen in the schedule of fixed property.

The sum allowed for the services of the superintendent is a fixed salary of one hundred and twenty give pounds per annum and one and a half percent on the proceeds of wrecked property. The arrangement with the other nine as appears by the articles given, three pounds per month and twenty shillings for each wreck; they sign articles of agreement for one year, and if all parties are agreeable they can continue in the service as long as they remain so, three months notice being given when they wish to leave. One of the persons at present in the service has been there over ten years.

I shall now present with the specified objects of the commission, reserving any further comments or suggestions that may not seem required to be attached to the different subjects as they are touched upon, to form the conclusion of this report, and shall commence with the wreck of the Schooner Fulton.

Special Report of the Schooner Fulton

The Fulton *lies about five miles from the principal station and about one mile from the West End of the Island.*

On reaching her I found her lying on a bank at the side of the channel that forms an outlet from the lake to the ocean, quite upright and at a sufficient distance from the beach surf, so as to be generally beyond its influence; and nearly in the same place as where the crew and passengers left the Island, or when the superintendent wrote respecting her.

I am of opinion that she might lie where she is now for months without further injury unless by some very extraordinary gale.

In proof of the safety of her position it may be said, that although she lies at nearly right angles to the beach, with her stern out, and which could of course receive the weight of any sea that could reach her, the rudder, which is still on her, is nearly as perfect as the day it was shipped when new, neither brace or bristle being in the least started.

I found the Fulton *to be a new vessel and since my return to the city have learned that she was launched at Baltimore in the United States in October last and is one hundred and ninety four tons burthen. She is of beautiful model, copper fastened and coppered.*

On examining her outside I found there was something less than three feet of water alongside of her at low tide, she being settled in the sand about a foot by the weight of the cargo. From nearly the waters edge at low tide up to her rails on both sides there is not an injury to be detected, excepting about the main chains on the starboard side where the plank is somewhat started, but not sufficient to alter her shear. I looked at her from the back on the beach and her sheer is as perfect as the day she was planked.

On the starboard side from about the water's edge downward as far as I could see, and nearly on the same line of futtock as she is injured above and for a space of about six feet forward, the planks are somewhat started and the oakum worked out of the beams, but in no worse further down than is to be seen, could be easily repaired. On the starboard side as far as can be seen down at the lowest tide there is no sign of injury, excepting the copper under the water being rubbed off for about eight or ten feed by her forging over the sand.

On examining her deck I found her to be about ninety six feet in length from the foremast of the stern to the afterpart of the sternpost, and about one hundred feet over all, about twenty four feet beams from outside to outside. The depth of hold I could not measure on account of the cargo being in her but should think about ten or eleven feet.

She had been fore and aft schooner rigged, the foremost which is over eighty feet still standing, the bowsprit is still in her with the stays complete, the jibboom run out, the fore gaff is on board and one topmast, and I believe the main boom and gaff are on the Island. She has a patent windlass now on board complete, the caboose house is on board and uninjured, there are two water casks on board of about two hundred and fifty gallons each, quite new, and said to have cost forty dollars. She has a very large trunk and a fine cabin.

The only injury to her deck is between the mainmast and main hatch, where it is hogged about six inches, and some appearance of straining in the starboard waterways. There can be no doubt the injury on the deck arises from an injury in the bottom which forced up the stanchions and with them three of the deck beams, one so much as to crack it. The way her lying on a knoll of sand or some other hard substance which causes that, if so, she will resume her shape when she floats. The extent of the injury to her bottom could not be seen from the outside on account of the sand, nor on the inside until the cargo is discharged. The injury in her bottom is sufficient for the tide to partially flow into her, yet I do not think it is sufficiently serious to prevent her being repaired and made as good a vessel or nearly so as she was before stranding. At high water she is about half full and at low tide there is not much water in her.

With the exception of some twenty barrels herring and about twenty quintals of codfish taken out of her before she was sold and partly used by the passengers, the cargo was in her that she left Newfoundland with and consisted of 560 barrels herring, 500 quintals codfish, about two tons of old slunk for paper, and two casks copper, weighing when they were put on board (as the mate informed me) nine hundred weight each. Note: There is not the least difficulty in saving the cargo, as boats can go alongside at all times of tide and receive the cargo and ship it much more conveniently than could be done off the beach. The herrings will all be saved, some not in good order, nearly all the codfish will be damaged, the slunk cannot injure. The two casks copper and two hundred barrels herring, some slunk, and a small lot of codfish, have already been brought to the city and disposed of for about one hundred and seventy pounds.

I am of opinion there will be no great difficulty in getting her off as soon as the cargo is out, and she would not have to be moved over one hundred yards to a place where there could be sufficient repairs on her to bring her to Halifax.

As respects the value of the Fulton, I am not prepared to state positively, she being a foreign bottom, I am not aware what difficulty there may be in getting a register. The hull when new I should think must have cost at least five thousand dollars and if she is not more injured than I think she is, should say she is worth — at least — as she lays, about four hundred pounds, if a register can be obtained for her without much cost.

Note: there was also a large quantity of cigars on board which were all damaged.

William Williams

As respects William Williams, I have to report that after due enquiry from himself and the superintendent, I learned that he is about fourteen years of age, without parents, left Liverpool clandestinely in the American ship Milo, stranded on the Island on or about the 14th December 1846. That when the crew were about leaving the Island, he asked the Superintendent to allow him to remain and live with him; that he has not been detained against his will, and that he did not wish to leave the Island before I asked him if he wanted to do so. I also learned that he received no wages, and he informed me that he had not been ill treated.

I brought him off with me agreeable to instructions, as he wishes to leave.

William Etter

With respect to William Etter, I was informed by the superintendent that he was sent to the Island in the spring of 1834 at the desire of his friends and with the consent of the then commissioner. That he has never been hired as a labourer, has never been considered as one of the Establishment, and that the Hon. William of Black pays Capt. Darby fifteen pounds a year for taking care of him.

From other sources I have learned that the commission received a note from the late Hon. JN Jeffrey, then administrator of the government, requesting them to permit Mr. Etter to proceed to the Island for the purpose of remaining with the superintendent in the capacity of schoolmaster or in any other situation that might be agreed upon.

I have also been informed that it was agreed with the parties who sent him there that fifteen pounds a year was to be allowed the Establishment, besides the fifteen pounds to be paid to Mr. Darby.

I am also informed by the superintendent that for the first ten years Etter was extremely violent and troublesome, and that very harsh measures had to be adopted towards him. That for the last four years he has been quiet, inoffensive and useful, and is now employed carrying wood and water, and otherwise doing the drudgery of the kitchen.

I am further informed by the superintendent that he has no authority to detain him; that he has taken care of him at the desire of the said Mr. Etter's friends, and is quite willing he should leave the Island at any time.

I questioned Etter as to his leaving the Island and he expressed a wish to do so, but in so identical a manner that I questioned him no further. I state it as my opinion, that his mind is so much disordered that no rational answer can be had from him.

That he has been detained on the Island against his will, I have no doubt. He is, I should think, kindly treated now, but the harsh treatment he formerly received has broken him down to the pitiable creature he now is.

If his intellect was disturbed when he was sent there, it was the wrong place to have sent him. Kind treatment might have restored his reason, but a long period of hardship has made him — I am afraid — a confirmed imbecile. I am of the opinion that his case requires a full investigation, much that I have heard of the treatment he has received I cannot bring myself to believe and trust it will prove unfounded. That he ought to be taken off the

Island without delay does not admit of a question.

This story adds a confusing and disturbing chapter to Sable Island's history. William Etter was never mentioned in Darby's journals, and his presence seemed to have been minimally recorded. The truth about his story — who these "friends" were that sent him to the island, including the "Hon. William of Black" that maintained him, why Darby allowed him to come, and what his treatment was actually like during the years he resided there — are lost. However, if Etter was sent to the island due to his mental illness or disability, this can at least give some insight to the limited options for care that people in his position had at the time. Looking at the fact that thirty pounds were being spent each year to keep him on the island, and that he was sent there to take on the respectable title of 'schoolmaster' (which he ostensibly never actually held) instead of being housed in an institution in the city, it seems likely that he came from a well-off family that perhaps thought shipping him away from the mainland was a better option than those in Halifax. In hosting Etter on the island, Darby was following in the footsteps of the old superintendent Michael Wallace, who was noted to have done the same thing for others.

As a result of this report, a few years later in 1853 a woman named Dorothea Dix came to Sable Island. She was an American lobbyist for the rights of mentally ill people, and had heard that people were being detained against their will on the island — likely from Townsend's report. She didn't find any evidence of this practice, which appeared to ceased. However, Dix saw a need for improved lifeboats on the island, and had new supplies sent to Sable Island which were immediately put to use, saving many lives within days of arrival.

Three years after her visit to Sable Island, Dorothea Dix and Halifax's mayor Hugh Bell began the construction of the Mount Hope Asylum. It opened the following year, and while it was a long way off from modern approaches to mental health support and management, it was the first facility of its kind in the province, and an alternative to the poorhouse for certain people with mental illness. In 1858 the government passed the "Act for the Management of the Hospital for the Insane", which was the new name of the institution. This act solidified the importance of the humane treatment of people with mental illness. Townsend's report may have had a small part in attracting attention to this issue, and in bringing Dix's attention to Nova Scotia in the first place.

The report continues, moving on to discuss the properties and assets on the island.

<u>*Schedule of Fixed Property at Sable Island*</u>

<u>*Principal Station or Head Quarter*</u>
The principal station or head quarter is situated about six miles from the West and on the north side of the Island, the large supply of fresh water in the immediate vicinity was the principal reason for fixing upon that spot.

There are here three large dwelling houses in good order, one occupied by the superintendent Mr. Joseph Darby and family, consisting of seven persons in all and all the persons employed on the Island except the two outpost men, and being generally about seven exclusive of the superintendent, and eight including Mr. Etter.

The other two houses are unoccupied and are kept ready for casualties. The two are capable of accommodating from one hundred to one hundred fifty persons, and more if necessity requires it.

There is a large barn and stables combined, with two large sheds in good order attached to them, the stable requires some repair. The whole are capable of accommodating about fifty head of cattle and containing about thirty tons of hay.

A wreckhouse fifty four feet long by eighteen feet wide, in good order.

A small warehouse, twenty feet by fourteen, in good order.

A workshop with blacksmiths forge in one end, in all about forty five feet long by eighteen feet wide, in good order.

A provision store twenty eight feet by twenty with a loft above, in good order.

Also fourteen outhouses of various sizes and for various uses.

Oil house, smoke house, wash house for transient persons, and houses for stock, vegetables, boats, etc.

An old building not worth repairing and at present used for making shingles.

Close to the superintendent's dwelling is the flag staff, with steps leading to the top which is sixty five feet high, and on top of which is the look out, being about now one hundred and twenty to one hundred and thirty feet above the level of the sea. The look out commands an excellent view of the Island and of the ocean in nearly all directions. This structure is a good mark for vessels at a distance on visiting the Island and would have cost considerable labor in erecting it.

This completes the fixed property at this station. The buildings at this station in case of emergency could accommodate four hundred persons.

<u>East End of the Lake Station</u>

This station is about nine miles to the Eastward of the principal station.

There is here one dwelling house, very old and in bad order, it is occupied by John Stevens, his wife and child and another female.

A barn and stable in good order, will accommodate about twenty-five heads of cattle, and contain fifteen tons of hay.

A warehouse about forty by thirty four feet in good order.

A workshop and three small outhouses.

A new dwelling house of large size is much wanted here. Should a large number of persons be wrecked in this vicinity in the winter season, I am of the opinion that there would be much suffering from want of room before they could be sent to headquarters. The present dwelling is very small and I should say quite unfit to reside in during the winter.

A flag staff and lookout complete the fixed property here.

East End Station

This station is about five miles to the Eastward of the East End of the Lake Station, and about four miles from the eastpoint of the Island, at the end of which is a dry beach about three miles in length.

At this station there is a good dwelling house which, with the exception of the roof requiring shingling, is in good order. It is occupied by *John Nesbitt*, his wife and six children.

A warehouse forty feet by twenty four in excellent order and the best on the Island.

A barn and stable in good order, and capable of accommodating about fifteen.

William Whitstone

As respects other persons placed on the Island, I am informed by the superintendent that the only other person placed there under similar circumstances was a *William Whitstone*, sent to the Island by his friends, with the consent of the then commissioner the late Hon. Michael Wallace, and taken off the next summer, being there about nine months.

Charles Lawson resided there about three months, and the superintendent informed me that he came and went off at his own pleasure.

Schedule of Moveable Property on Sable Island

Principal Station or Headquarters

35 head of horned cattle of which 11 are milk cows
8 working horses with harness in bad order
6 sets new harness made to replace old
6 riding horses with 5 saddles - for the use of the men going to wrecks, going rounds of the Island in thick weather, etc.
13 pigs, 10 large and 3 small
6 geese, about 40 fowls
1 life boat with gear complete and in excellent order

5 boats with gear complete and in good order
1 punt, in good order
1 large scow, wanting some repairs
1 hay wagon, wanting some repairs
5 carts, all in good order
1 truck, all in good order
3 sleds, all in good order
2 harrows, all in good order
6 hay forks, 6 hay rakes, 3 dung forks
1 boat wagon, when separated makes two carts for various purposes
1 cart body, complete
1 wheel barrow
1 bait mill
3 boat sails
19 1/2 shingles of good quality, made on the island, about 3000 feet pine lumber and scantling

<u>Contained in Store House</u>
10 barrels pork sent to the Establishment
1 1/2 barrels pork, island cure
3 barrels beef, island cure
2 barrels beef from Halifax (bad) to be returned
5 barrels Herrings
2 barrels mackerel
9 barrels salt and about 10 salt in bulk
Codfish, sufficient for summer
2 barrels sugar
1 barrel molasses
19 barrels bread
21 barrels flour
2 barrels oatmeal
4 barrels corn meal
1/2 barrel coffee
1 barrel rice

1/2 barrel peas
1/2 barrels barley
1/2 barrel porter, saved from frigate Barbados *wrecked in 1813*
1 1/2 kegs powder
1 bag shot 1/4 left
3 puncheons soldiers coats
4 scythes, new
3 draw knives, new
8 axes, new
1/2 box glass
2 keg white lead
1/2 keg salt petre
1 steel yard
1 long composition plate
1 composition rudder gudgeon

<u>In Oil House</u>
2 large iron pots and gear for trying out oil

<u>In several house adjoining</u>
9 bars steel
a lot of old copper
a lot panel doors from Barque Detroit
2 setts copper hinges
1 Franklin stove - old

<u>In Workshop</u>
2 jack screws
1 grindstone
2 whip saws
1 cross-cut saw
2 handed awl
15 fathom half wick chair
5 bars heavy iron

1 bundle small iron
12 bundles sloop iron
6 rod steel
1 vice, 1 anvil, 1 pair bellows
1 forge hammer
2 broad axes
1 maul
1 lot of augers - poor
7 chopping axes
9 shovels
4 draw knives
1 hand hammer
1 chest containing sundry tools
1 ships winch
1 grapnel
1 large gun

<u>In Smoke Houses</u>
1 Franklin stove
1 square stove (broken)
1 barrel lime
1 small lot bricks

<u>In Warehouse</u>
60 sheets new copper

<u>In little warehouse</u>
4 empty water casks
12 barrels bait

<u>At Dwelling House</u>
1 stomach pump and injection pipe, complete
1 Tooth Drawer
1 medicine chest, incomplete
1 doz skein twine

1/2 doz splitting knives
1 doz handsaw files
1/4 chest tea
1 square stove, nearly new
1 ensign
5 old muskets
1 sky glass, has been on the island since 1803
23 volumes books, presented by Bishop Ingles
1 piece sole leather
14 life preservers
10 rugs
6 pair sheets, 3 pair blankets, 7 pillows - small (old and much worn)
a lot of cotton canvas
2 bake oven, 4 good pots, 2 tea kettles
1 doz milk pans, 10 tin pints
2 tables

<u>*At the Flag Staff*</u>
1 12 pounder carronade

<u>*East End of Lake Station*</u>
3 horses and harness
3 cows
3 yearlings
3 sheep - property of John Stevens
6 Geese, 12 Fowls
1 good boat with gear complete
1 life belt
1 cart, in good order
1 carronade
1 axe, 1 shovel
2 hoes, 1 scythe
3 hay forks, 1 dung fork, 4 hay rakes
1 bake oven, 1 tea kettle, 1 large pot

3 milk pans, 6 tin pints
1 square stove, nearly new
1/2 hand fish
1/2 hand flour
1/2 hand meal

<u>East End Station</u>
1 good boat with gear complete
3 horses and harness, complete
2 cows, 2 pigs
1 good cart
1 large bake pan, 1 tea kettle
3 earthen pans, 6 tin pints
3 tables
1 axe, 1 scythe
2 hay forks, 1 dung fork
1 shovel, 3 hay rakes

<u>Sundries ready to be shipped belonging to the Establishment</u>
27 barrels oil
12 barrels mackerel
6 barrels hides
46 bars steel
a lot of bolt and sheet copper
10 composition rudder braces and pintles
2 iron rudder braces
a quantity of old iron
a quantity of old lead
a quantity of old junk
12 barrels herrings
a quantity of dry fish, part of cargo of Sch. Fulton

Note. the life, and all the other boats, with the exception of one, and all the carts and wagons, except one cart, have been built on the Island under the present superintendent.

Description of wrecks and wrecked property on and about Sable Island with their ownership, commencing at the Principal Station and thence eastward, on the north side.

"Eliza". Eastward from the flag staff about four and a half miles lie the remains of the Barque Eliza *of Pictou, stranded in 1840. Fit only for fuel, had but little copper in her at present being broken up.*

"Milo". One and a half miles Eastward from the Eliza *are the remains of the American ship* Milo *of Portsmouth N.S. coppered and copper fastened, was stranded in December 1846, lies about one hundred and fifty fathoms from the beach. Tops of timber just awash. Is supposed to have about 600 tons of iron in her and belongs to Mr G. Paw and others.*

"Louisa". About a pistol shot distant westwardly of the mile is about the spot where the Schooner Louisa *of Sydney C.B. was stranded in November 1842. A box containing money was east from her. Her hull has been broken up.*

"Detroit". Four miles eastward from ship Milo *lies the hull of the American Barque* Detroit *of Bath, stranded September 1846. She is very little injured and lies nearly dry at low water, is coppered and copper fastened, masts standing, bowsprit and jibboom out, one anchor on the bow chain plates still on her and complete and hawsepipes in: belongs to the Establishment. Although this vessel had been lying there over a year and a half, no attempt had been made to strip her of those articles. The copper was still on her bottom, with the exception of what had been washed off, and the composition gudgeon and pintles still on her. I am of the opinion that if the caps, tops, chain plates, bob stays, hawsepipes, copper, rudder pintles and the anchor had been taken off and sent to Halifax they would have realized from seventy five to one hundred pounds. On bringing it to the notice of the superintendent, they stripped off all the copper that could be got at and had taken off the composition pintles and gudgeons while I remained on the Island and were at work at the chain plates. Her hull would be valuable to break up for fuel on account of the*

copper and iron in her.

"*Barbados*". *Four and a half miles to the Eastward of the* Detroit *and directly opposite the East End Station lie the remains of the British Frigate* Barbados, *stranded in 1812. She is entirely under water and has not been seen for years; her whole armament is buried with her. There is a keg of powder still on the Island saved from her.*

"*Levant*". *About half a mile from the East end of the Island on the south side of the bar lie the remains of the ship* Levant *of St John NB of 800 tons; stranded in August 1847. Copper fastened, is nearly all under water, has all her chain plates on, one anchor on the bows and one under bows, each weighing about 29 cwt belonged to Mr Henry Boggs.*

"*Eagle*". *About three miles westwardly from the east end and on the south side lie the remains of the American ship* Eagle *of New York stranded in August 1835. Is at present covered with sand, is about twenty yards from the shore. Had valuable cargo left in her, one article of which was twenty five tons of sheet copper: by the working and shifting of the sand this may appear.*

"*Courser*". *About four miles to the westward of the* Eagle *lie the remains of the American ship* Courser *of Portsmouth, stranded in 1830. Has not been seen for years, had a valuable cargo in her, much of which is likely there yet and may wash up. Belongs to Mr. Edward Wallace.*

"*Orpheus*". *About two miles westward of the remains of the* Courser *and abreast of the East and of the Lake Station on the south side, lie the remains of the Brigantine* Orpheus *of Bermuda, stranded in 1831. Cedar built and copper fastened. Her remains are buried in the sand high on the beach. She is owned by Mr. Edward Wallace. * See remark at the end of the report.*

"*Triumph*". *Close to the remains of the* Orpheus *lie the remains of the Brig* Triumph *of Windsor, stranded in the fall of 1841, partly visible. Iron fastened, of but little value. Owned by the Establishment.*

"*Blooming Youth*". *About one mile from the remains of the*

Triumph *lies the hull of the American fishing schooner* Blooming Youth *of Gloucester, stranded in April 1840, hull entire, lies high on the beach, is copper spiked: belongs to the Establishment.*

"Marmora". *About one mile westward of the* Blooming Youth *lie the remains of the American ship* Marmora *of Richmond Virginia, stranded in 1841. Copper fastened, she is about twenty yards from the beach, sternpost visible at low water. Is the property of the Island.*

"Adelphi". *About six miles westward of the remains of the* Marmora *are the remains of the British brig* Adelphi, *stranded in 1828. About two thirds of her are on the beach and the remainder in the water, visible at low tide. Was loaded with pine timber, out of which a very large quantity of ships were made for the present owner of her. She was thoroughly copper fastened. Property of Mr. Edward Wallace and Mr. Joseph Darby.*

"L'Africane". *About two miles westward of the remains of the* Adelphi *is the spot where the French Frigate* L'Africane *was stranded in 1822, her remains lie about three quarters of a mile from the shore in about two and a half fathoms water, her whole armament lies there with her remains.*

"Maria". *About one mile to the westward of the remains of* L'Africane *and in the mouth of the old opening on the south side is the spot where the French Barque* Maria *of Havre was stranded in 1839. No part of her hull is remaining. I note the place where she was last as there was a large amount of specie lost with her.*

"Fulton". *On the north side of the Island about one mile from the west end lies the hull of the American Schooner* Fulton *of Baltimore, of nearly 200 tons, stranded on the 14th February 1848. A special account of her condition is attached to this report.*

These include all the wrecks on or about the Island that are visible or likely to be valuable; those that are stated as buried, are mentioned, so as to note the spot where they were last or are lying in the event of any part of them heaving up by the shifting of the sand in heavy gales as is quite probable might be the case.

The place where those that had specie in them were lost, as noted, as it may be worked up at some future time if it hasn't done so already.

The positions of the copper fastened vessels are noted so as if they should heave up on the beach they would be the most valuable to break up in the event of a scarcity of firewood.

The places where the remains of the frigate Barbados *and* L'Africane *are supposed to lie, are noted, more on account of their being ships of war than for any other reason.*

I would here ask leave to call the attention of the government to the propriety of different persons owning property on or about the island for all time, as already been the cause of some dispute and bad feeling and if it should so happen that any thing of value should be thrown on shore from any of the wrecks at any time, and which was each supposed to belong to certain individuals much trouble and confusion might arise.

I have been informed that the superintendent had, on being accused of disposing of copper belonging to the Establishment for his own benefit, come forward and declared that it was copper obtained from the wreck belonging to himself, meaning I believe, the Adelphi; the greater part of which wreck is on the beach and which vessel he informed me was singularly well copper fastened.

Admitting as we must do, without any proof against him that the copper so disposed of was "bona fide" his, the superintendent's own property, it might nevertheless leave doubts on the public mind, that their ought not to be the case, I think will generally be admitted. This source of suspicion ought to be removed.

I could therefore recommend (if it will not seem to be doing injustice) that all persons that may own wrecks or wrecked property in the Island or its shores shall have notice that the same must be removed within two years (lesser times can be given if that should not seem sufficient), and that all not removed within that time should become the property of the Establishment. If this plan should not meet approval some plan to make all the wrecked property on the Island or about its shores belong to the Establishment should be adopted.

I would also recommend in the sales of all future wrecks or wrecked property, that it shall be imperative to have it duly advertised and that no sale shall be legal without being so advertised, and that the commissioners be in possession of all the facts relating to such wreck or wrecks as may be for sale and be prepared to make them known at the time of such sale, or previously by public advertisement, and not to offer or cause to be offered any wreck or wrecks that may be on the Island until they are in possession of all the facts relating to them. And I would further recommend that two years be allowed to all future purchasers to remove any wrecks or wrecked property from off the Island or its shores and if not removed within the specified time that all such shall become the property of the Establishment.

<u>*Charges against Commissioners and Superintendents*</u>
In reference to the investigation I am required to make into the nature of the charges made by the commissioners against the superintendent, and of the complaints made by the superintendent against the commissioners. I have to state, that in all the documents handed to me there are but two specific charges made against the superintendent by the commissioners, their complaint being against his general conduct of late.

In their letter of 29th March of this year addressed to the Provincial Secretary, they refer to a report previously laid before His Excellency in which they assert there are charges which they are prepared to substantiate. A copy of that report I had not, and therefore could not question the superintendent in reference to those charges. In that letter they complain of his treatment of the passengers of the Fulton but do not state what that treatment was. I pointed out that charge to the superintendent and asked his reply to it; he answered me he knew of no ill treatment any of them had received and that passengers never left the Island better satisfied.

In the commissioners letter to the superintendent dated 1st April 1848 they charge him with a total silence respecting the state of the Schooner Fulton *and the prospect of saving her cargo;*

his answer to this was that he was so situated that he had not time to write fully respecting her. This answer was not satisfactory for I am of opinion that on reference to his letter of that date in which he speaks of the Fulton, it will be found that he had time to write about other matters, of not so much consequence as a full description of the Fulton would have been, as respects the interests of of the Establishment and all others concerned in her. The letter will speak for itself.

As respects the complaints of the superintendent against the commissioners in his letter to the Lieut. Governor dated 18th February 1848 I have to state that the complaints therein contained are so numerous and varied that it would occupy too much space to enter on them in this report, and beg leave to recommend that for the sake of Justice to all parties, the request of the commissioners be acceded to, and that the superintendent be ordered to Halifax, so that a full and fair investigation may be catered into touching all matters and disputes between them, and would further recommend, that while the superintendent is in the city, there should be an enquiry into the management of the affairs of the Island generally. I am of opinion that this is absolutely necessary, for the many reports in circulation and the assertions of some of the men now on the Island and others that have been there are injurious to the character of the Establishment and of the superintendent, and ought to be investigated and refuted if untrue.

Employment of Persons belonging to the Establishment

As respects the enquiry into the Employment of the men belonging to the Establishment, I would by leave to refer to the journal kept daily, and returned to the commissioners quarterly. It is there noted what they are daily employed at, but as it may not be convenient for the journal to follow this report, I will write the leading employments.

When there are any wrecks on the Island, all hands are of service employed about them, at other times they are employed *collecting and hauling wood, which occupies much time; two men are generally employed about the stock and house. At this season they are principally employed in farming, in the fall harvesting, and in general in keeping the premises and boats in order. In foggy weather two men are sent daily round the shores of the Island to look out for wrecks. There is no doubt time to spare which would be turned to account were the present system of remuneration altered. Most of the men at present employed are quite dissatisfied and they generally leave as soon as their time is up.*

In a place like the Island where it is a kind of expatriation to live, sufficient encouragement might be given to induce the best men to go there. If there is much wrecking — in winter especially — it is laborious work and requires strong, active, hardy men; any other would be broke up in a few days.

The present system of monthly wages only is not attended with the best results; the men employed are certain of the amount agreed upon whether they do little or much; there is no stimulus to exertion beyond what may be considered the routine business of the Establishment. They are allowed, it is true, twenty shillings for every wreck; that they expect to get whether the wreck realizes one pound or one hundred, and, in the winter especially, it is hard to get men to exert themselves as much as they might without that powerful lever "self interest".

I therefore strongly recommend that out of the proceeds of all property disposed of, that is required by the labor of the persons employed on the Island, a certain percentage should be set apart to be divided among the persons so employed in addition to their stated wages, which I think under this system might be reduced. The sum to be received by each person as a percentage not to exceed a certain amount in each year.

With this system in operation the best men would be obtained, and would be anxious to remain here, and I am of opinion it would be a means of materially increasing the funds of the Establishment.

Allowance to Transient Persons

I would also beg leave to call attention to the provisions at present allowed to persons who may be thrown upon the Island. The only allowance — the superintendent informed me — that the regulations of the Island sanction to transient persons is one pound of salt beef or pork and one pound of bread or flour per day, for men, and a reduced allowance of the same for women and children. This allowance I should think quite insufficient for hearty, healthy men and not at all suitable for the generality of women and children; it has been the source of much discomfort and trouble and I am of opinion ought to be remedied.

Instead of the salt meats for the women and children I would recommend that oatmeal, corn meal or rice, and tea and sugar be substituted, and to be given to those who preferred them in certain quantities at the discretion of the superintendent. Although not within his province so to do, I believe the superintendent had on his own responsibility at certain times allowed tea and sugar etc. to transient persons.

Visits to the Island

I would also recommend that the Island should be visited at stated times, say once a month, if the cost of doing so is not found to be too great. The benefit to the Island of fixed and stated visits will be obvious. About a year and a half since there were three crews and some passengers on the Island at the time, some of whom were there nearly eighty days: had the Island been visited monthly, a large saving of provisions would have been one of the results.

As there is no stated time for visiting the Island, the superintendent as well as the persons whom accident may place there, are kept in complete suspense as to the arrival of any vessel. If there were stated visits — no matter how many — it would be a great comfort to persons when accident places there to know when they could get off the Island.

Should the visits be monthly so large a stock of perishable stores need not be kept. At present there is a six months stock on hand — with the exception of some groceries — the flour therefore will likely turn sour before it is used.

With monthly visits or once every two months, much more than half the present stock need be kept on hand. At any rate whatever the number of visits may be, let them be at stated times and known to all interested.

The last recommendation that I have to offer in this report is that one or more of the commissioners visit the Island twice at least in every year, and learn for themselves the requirements and working of the Establishment.

In conclusion I have to add that in the foregoing report I have endeavoured to give all the facts and information that the short notice I had of proceeding to the Island and my limited stay there have enabled me to give and trust I shall be excused any errors or omissions.

All of which is respectfully submitted.
William T. Townsend.
Halifax, Nova Scotia
26 April 1848

Since making the foregoing report my attention having been called by Mr. Wallace to the fact that the "Courser" and "Orpheus" were purchased by him previous to his being appointed a commissioner, and the brig "Adelphi" was also purchased by himself and Mr. Joseph Darby previous to their being officially connected with the Establishment.
12 January 1849
William T Townsend

"I have seldom found a more satisfactory document," was the note that Joseph Howe left on the report Townsend submitted. This lengthy and detailed report proved Townsend was the right person for this job; his knowledge of ships and the shipping business meant that he could speak accurately to the many details of the wrecks and their value, and he had no trouble asking Darby the difficult questions required by the charges laid against him.

Townsend made many recommendations, and though they were not all acted upon, they demonstrated an acute understanding of the problems that Darby faced in running the island. He highlighted the difficulty in finding dedicated employees, and the ways in which their salaries could be restructured in order to entice them to work harder. He determined the current rules for providing food for stranded persons to be insufficient, and combined with a lack of scheduled visits to the island, the situation regarding provisions and resources to be unreasonable for anyone to manage. This confirmed one of Darby's long-standing complaints, and shone more light on the accusations of cruelty made toward Darby, most of which centred around strict rations.

These untenable situations were either unknown, ignored, or underestimated by the commissioners. Townsend also pointed out a major cause for this problem: the commissioners never visited Sable Island themselves. He recommended that each commissioner be required to visit the island twice a year, or on another regular schedule. The combination of the superintendent being required to follow unreasonable regulations, and the commissioners being completely out of touch with the realities of life on Sable, meant that a conflict such as this was inevitable. Change had to take place on Sable Island.

Two weeks after this report was submitted, one of the commissioners, W. Cunard, resigned from his position.

> *Halifax, 13th May 1848*
> *Sir,*
> *From recent indisposition and confirmed declining health, I am induced to request that you will be pleased to bring to the notice of His Excellency the Lieut. Governor, my desire to resign from the appointment as one of the commissioners for Sable Island, the duties of which I feel unable longer to attend.*
> *I am, Sir, your most obd. serv.*
> *W. Cunard*
> *To the Honbl. Joseph Howe*
> *Provincial Secretary*

Cunard left the two remaining commissioners to finish the affair, and to try and preserve their reputations throughout.

In order to make their case, the commissioners began compiling whatever evidence they could that Darby was to blame for the mismanagement of the island. This included the testimonial of John Nesbitt, who wrote a letter from Sable Island's East End station.

East End Sable Island, 14th May 1848
Dear Sir,
I thought when I left Halifax to come to this Island, I was coming to a place of peace and happiness for my self and my family, but the contrary has been the case, that I am entirely wore out and oppressed to the lowest degree with the unprincipled tyrannical and diabolical treatment of the superintendent, particularly these last twelve months, or since the repairing and fitting up of the Schooner Lady Echo, *when no one could please him, but damn this one and damn that one continually, that I left him and walk home, every one doing their very utmost for him and his family, that for many days the men was not allowed to go to dinner till night although not a quarter mile distance. All this was considered nothing if he was only satisfied, but he could never get enough done, which that vessel almost or entirely ought to belong to the Establishment of this Island. The next thing, he mocked me personally about was at the wreck of the* Levant, *when all hands knocked off wrong the wreck, there was considerable left on board. Mr. Darby and all his men went home intending not to return until the cutter came. Captain Reid was here and three or four of his crew, heard ask me if I would get my team and go down to assist him in getting the remains of the materials on there, that there might be no delay when the cutter comes. I went and we succeeded in getting all on there, five boat loads. I hauled them where the rest of the materials was, hauled up the boat and came home. This was Saturday night. On Monday morning the cutter commenced loading. All was on board before sunset. When all was over Darby had learned that the remains of the materials had been brought from the wreck.*

He then attacked me with disobedience of orders. He told me I had no right to go there without being sent to save any materials, that he would report my conduct to the commissioners, and have me turned off the Island immediately. I told him very calmly I thought I was here for the purpose of saving wrecked property. He damned me and the wrecked property and said I had no business to go there without his orders. After he took his satisfaction of abusing me, I told him he might report me to the commissioners or whom he pleased. I learned directly afterwards he had been advising his sons to purchase the wreck so he thought of getting a greater haul if their materials had been left on board. For he never intended to assist in getting any thing more on shore. Two or three weeks after this, the Lady Echo *landed here from Halifax. Nothing on board to eat. John Darby asked me if I could supply them. There happened to be some hard bread here and a few other articles we would not have had, only the men being all lately here from the West End, I gave them what I could share to keep them from starving, and they proceeded. But after that they took another thought and went up to the West End Establishment and got fully victualled. Mr. Darby came down next day with all hands to load the vessel. He began at me for caring to give away the provisions. I demonstrated with him of them starving to death, I told him they might as well get it at one end of the Island as another. He seemed very much agitated that I should be led into the secret, and abused me very much pleading up his own honesty. Next voyage the* Lady Echo *came it was the same thing. No provisions on board, I had to take my cart to the North East Bar with all we could spare of our pitiful allowance to keep them from starving until they could get to the West End by Mr. Darby's orders.*

As soon as we were done wrecking last year, poor Nichols case came on. He fled from the wrath and blows of Darby down to me, he was in a very bad state indeed, his legs were all broke out in sores and as red as scarlet from the hips to the heels. I done all I could for him and took him back to the West End. He came down twice afterwards, being starved out. I gave him all the necessaries

I could share to keep him from actual starvation. He was a good useful man for this Establishment but very unjustly and very severely treated. Ever since that transaction happened, Darby has given me no peace, but abusing me and calling me every abusive name that his scandalous tongue can use, every time I go to the West End, for harbouring that Nichols and not horsewhipping him back to his post. Our usage is very different indeed, we have been six months at one time and four months at another time, that we have never seen milk or butter and other things scant enough, although there are five cows at Stevens place and I believe fifteen at the West End. We have never had but one and that dry half the time. The day Mr. Townsend landed on the Island he gave us another cow, I suppose out of policy or shame. Even the rum that comes on, we scarcely get one third of our share. It is sold for those that will pay for it. One man told me, that had only been eight months here, he had bought six gallons of rum and another four and so on. There is no man has any business here that knows anything, he will get very little peace. His relations and a few half Indians and black men from Country Harbour answers him best. He can make them put their cross to every document he writes and swear to it afterward. He has now got on his niece and her husband from Country Harbour waiting for the first vacancy of an outpost. Indeed I think Darby has had his day, he has filled his pockets well, and the measure of his abominations are pretty well filled up. Even those that have kept him in office. He is sounding in our ears continually about the conduct of them damned infernal commissioners that has robbed this Island. He says the name of a Wallace he loves, but Edward Wallace as a commissioner he hates with a perfect hatred, for he is a damned rascal. His tongue never ceases to abuse the commissioners, he says only for his industry this Establishment would have become a wreck long ago.

It takes one man to make shoes, another to shoot ducks, another to make chests and trunks, and another besides old Billy Etter to attend to the house affairs, besides all hands employed a great part of the time either directly or indirectly for the benefit of him and his family. This, as far as I have seen, has been his chief industry, and as for his own doings, I have never seen him do any thing but talk. There is not a man here ever saw him get a foot wet any more than a cat would. It is in vain for me to write you any more. I suppose you are pretty well aware of it all. There is one thing, if he is not removed I must leave the Island as soon as possible. With a clean conscience, I would willingly make oath to all I have stated. His own brother-in-law has told me enough to transport him beyond the seas. Sir I hope you will excuse me for taking the liberty of writing you on the subject for I am necessitated. I have written you to please send me a spy glass as it is very inconvenient to be without one.

I remain your most ardent and humble servant,
John Nesbitt
E. Wallace, Esquire
Commissioner for Sable Island

Nesbitt's letter would have provided the commissioners with all they could have hoped for. It gave testimony of Darby's temper, his ill-will towards the commissioners, and accounts of various misdoings from a point of view that supported the commissioners' charges. Most of Nesbitt's complaints stem from issues surrounding food distribution, which has been well established as a great point of stress for Darby. Nesbitt sounded quite tender-hearted, handing out whatever food he had to anyone asking for it. Removed as he was from the main station, he may have been unaware of the scarcity of food during certain parts of the year.

The points that he made regarding Darby's family members and his nepotism are interesting. As Townsend confirms in his report, the island has a consistent problem of attracting employees that could handle the physical toll of the work, and who were willing to work for the wages offered. Some of the most long-standing men working for Darby were members of his own family: his brother-in-law John Stevens, and his sons John and James. It was unsurprising that in light of this, he would seek to hire more members of his family, such as his niece and her husband as Nesbitt mentioned. Family members were likely to be more loyal and obedient, and these were two qualities that Darby valued in his workers.

Nesbitt's testimony painted a fairly unflattering picture of Darby's actions and temperament, and his statements were later addressed by Darby himself, where they were explained and rationalised. However, Nesbitt also cast doubt on the validity of any testimonies that Darby might procure, insinuating that he would write them himself and make others sign them.

In the end, this document wasn't enough to protect the positions of the commissioners. They had already been found wanting enough to merit their dismissal. In an otherwise uninteresting letter the following week, commissioners Cunard and Lawson speak of their roles as commissioners in the past tense, indicating that they are no longer serving in this capacity.

> *Halifax, 20th May 1848*
> *Sir,*
> *During the period of our service as Commissioners of Sable Island, it became necessary for us to give bonds to the admiralty for a quantity of iron ballast for the use of the Schooner "Daring".*
> *This bond apprehends a personal liability on our part. We beg to ask the favour of His Excellency, the Lieutenant Governor, that he will be pleased to order that the same may be transferred to our successors in office, or that one may be released from any penalties attending to it.*
> *We have the honor to be, Sir, your most obedient servants,*
> *E Cunard*
> *W Lawson Junior*
> *To the Honorable Joseph Howe*
> *Provincial Secretary*

The commissioners were all removed from their posts. There never were any successors, as this letter assumes. The lieutenant governor's office was clearly frustrated with this system of management and reassigned the business of Sable Island to the Board of Works in Halifax. The superintendent would now correspond with the chairman of this board, and matters would be deliberated by a committee, rather than by a few private individuals.

It remained to be seen, however, whether Joseph Darby would continue to serve as the superintendent, or if a new person would be appointed to the role. If Darby continued in his role, he would have been in a position of significant advantage over the members of the Board of Works, being far more experienced in the island's affairs.

Darby was summoned to Halifax to provide his testimony to the charges laid against him. He wrote to Harvey's office, amenable to doing so, and stood firmly by his own innocence.

> *Sable Island, 7th June 1848*
> *To His Excellency, Lieut. General, Sir John Harvey, Knight of the Grand Crop, of the most Honourable Military Order of the Bath; Lieut. Governor, and Commander in Chief, in, and over the Province of Nova Scotia and its dependencies.*
> *May it please your Excellency:*
> *Being directed by a letter from the Commissioners of Sable Island, dated the first day of June 1848, to proceed to the Capital of the Province for the purpose of giving such information of the management and condition of the Establishment which I superintend as might be required by the government, or the commissioners, I hastened to embark on board the Schooner* Daring, *the means of conveyance provided, so as to reach the Capital on or about the 12th following. I have also in conformity to the instructions of the commissioners directed Mr. John Nesbitt to embark on board the* Daring *without loss of time, and to be in attendance upon the commissioners at Halifax. I have ordered Mr. John Stevens (in charge of the East End of the Lake establishment), deeming him the most competent to the trust, to assume the care of the Establishment during my absence, and leaving him full instructions for his guidance, at the same time impressing upon the people the necessity of implicit obedience to all the lawful commands that he, as their superior, may see proper to*

give during my absence.

I have taken care to ship by the Daring *the property belonging to the Island already reported, as ready to be shipped, also such stores as are deemed unfit for use that they may be replaced by others.*

In the communication I have received from the commissioners of Sable Island, touching the wreck of the Schooner Fulton and the prospect of saving any part of her cargo, it is stated by the commissioners that the public have applied for information, and not only them but themselves as commissioners of Sable's property had a right to repeat, that all information should have been through me in the possession of Government. All that I can say is no regards to the state of the Fulton, and the prospect of saving any part of her cargo. I fully communicated to the commissioners in my letter of the 20th of March last, stating her condition as she then lay, but the gale of the 25th of March altered her position and rendered the prospects of saving the cargo much more favourable. They are pleased to state that they are willing to give to the superintendent all the praise to which his conduct has generally entitled him, yet they feel that they should be wanting in their duty did they not report that they had at times grave and serious charges brought against me. What those grave and serious charges are they do not particularize, therefore I am left without the possibility of an explanation, though fully conscious that whatever they may be, I could repel them and indicate my character, after being engaged in the public service during a period of forty years, diligently spent as I trust in the performance of duties incident to my situation. I hope your Excellency will pardon my little warmth of feeling at the imputations cast at my character in this advanced period of my life. And I beg your Excellency to believe that I would not approach the Representative of Majesty in my own vindication if I were not fully in possession of proof satisfactorily to vindicate my conduct and character from the charges and imputations by which I have been so falsely assailed, trusting that your Excellency will afford me an early opportunity of either in person or by memorial

of replying to any other charges of which I am not yet informed, and your memorialist as in duty bound will relate.
Joseph Darby
Superintendent of Sable Island

He boarded the ship where his son was captain and made the three day journey across the water to Halifax. This was an exceedingly rare event, as Darby never liked to leave the island unsupervised. However, once he was finally on the mainland Darby was able to get a copy of Townsend's report and read it for himself. It seemed that he was pleased with Townsend's impressions for the most part, offering only a short list of corrections. These notes were not all related to his charges, but simply notes to improve the accuracy of the document.

Halifax, 15th June 1848
Some remarks on Capt. Townsend's Report:
First, with regard to the Fulton being found in the same position as when last reported by the superintendent will bear a little explanation, as then when reported by the superintendent, she was laying on the bank where the sea at high water, or half tide, broke violently about her; but the gale on the 25th of March hove her inside the bank into smooth water where Captain Townsend found her, and between the 20th of March (the day she was reported) and the 25th (the day of the gale) no boat could get off the north side.
Second, as regards the water casks, when reported by the superintendent they were full of ice, and owing to their great weight they could not be moved.
Third, as regards to the £15 for Mr. Etter's board to be paid to the Island, I never heard a word of it before I saw it in Mr. Townsend's report, and his violent conduct had to be met with resolute resistance.
Fourth, the warehouse at the East End being the best on the Island: it was put up by the superintendent before Nesbitt went there.

> *Fifth, the remark about money being lost in the wreck of the Maria. It is possible that it may wash up at some future time, but it has never done so yet.*
>
> *Sixth, the letter describing the Fulton on the 20th of March was, I thought, quite sufficient, and the other matter, subject of the letter, was equally important, as a part of it was intended to save the commissioners from paying for a cask of beef.*
>
> *Seventh, the anchors, iron chain plates, and copper on the Detroit, could not have been easily got until quite lately, that the ship was hove up on the beach, but since that they have been able to get it.*
>
> *Eighth, where Mr. Townsend states that the superintendent informed him that there was but seventy head of horses there eighteen years ago, I beg leave to correct and say that there was but seventy head of horses on the Island when he went there first, forty one years ago.*
>
> *All of which I humbly beg leave to submit.*
>
> *Joseph Darby, Superintendent*
>
> *Captain Townsend also in remarking on the Fulton, quotes from the circumstance of her rudder not being broken, this is not a proper criterion to go by, as the rudders of many wrecks that I have known remain uninjured until the final breaking up of the whole of the vessel. Darby.*

As Darby found no further faults with Townsend's report and evaluation, and Joseph Howe declared it to be a quality document, there appeared to be little left to discuss. Feeling good about this turn of events, Darby prepared to return to the island and resume his position as superintendent. However, the following day, the final bit of damning evidence arrived from the departing commissioners, detailing everything they had gathered against Darby and listing their charges against him.

> *The commissioners of Sable Island feel great reluctance in bringing to the notice of the Government any complaint against the Superintendent of the Establishment, Capt. Joseph Darby,*

inasmuch as his general conduct in the management of it has hitherto, as far as their knowledge, with some exceptions, been satisfactory.

These exceptions have invariably received the requisite investigation on the part of the commission, and they had hoped that the approval given him on these occasions would have the effect of preventing a recurrence of any further deviation from his line of duty. The isolated position of the Island, the consequent infrequent opportunities of communicating with it, and the impossibility of ascertaining correctly how servants who are sometimes actuated by fear of offending, or a desire to injure or conciliate the superintendent, render it difficult to ascertain the exact truth of any information impartial to them with reference to the Island. Great reliance must necessarily be placed upon the character, integrity, and experience of the person placed in charge. The commissioners regret exceedingly that they now, from facts which have recently come to their knowledge, are compelled by an imperative sense of duty, to bring forward the following charges against the superintendent, which they hope he may be enabled to disprove and thus again render him worthy of their confidence.

The commissioners will therefore name in the first instance the case of Mr. Nesbitt. This man, a servant of the Establishment, forwarded last autumn a memorial (No. 1) to His Excellency who transmitted the same to the commissioners for their report. They recommended the payment of one half amount of his wages until an opportunity was afforded for the superintendent's reply. This reply consisted of documents No. 2-4. These documents, comprising the affidavit of Stevens, Mr. Darby's brother-in-law, and that of Martin Clye, and the statements purporting to be those of Graham, Morash, or Geller, and yet not signed by them, are considered by the commissioners very unsatisfactory, and they are of the opinion from the evidence of Mr. Nesbitt (No. 5) and Morash (No. 6) that the treatment of Mr. Nesbitt was wholly unjustifiable.

No. 2: The superintendent placed on the article of the Establishment his son, Thomas F.U. Darby, as cook, a boy of eleven years of age and wholly incapable of performing the duties assigned to him. That which renders this act much more reprehensible, is the circumstances of the name having been misstated — that of Thomas Fitzgerald having been used instead. Mr. Darby received the usual mens wages for this boy for 18 months, and claimed the customary compensation for wrecks, the payment of both of which was immediately stopped on the fact becoming known to the commissioners. An explanation was demanded and his reply (No. 7) is herewith submitted.

No. 3: The superintendent's treatment of Mr. John Nesbitt, placed in charge of the East End Establishment. His written statement (No. 5) will explain. He has also imparted orally further information to the commissioners which they think demands investigation and enquiry.

No. 4: The repetition of the illegal and improper act of selling liquor to the servants of the Establishment. His offence has been previously noted by the commissioners and Mr. Darby severely reprimanded therefore.

No. 5: The general disrespect evinced by Mr. Darby towards the commissioners as evidenced by his journal (No. 8), his letters (No. 9), and the testimony of Nesbitt, Morash, and Nichols. They do not make this a personal matter, but they deem it their duty to notice such conduct as tending to create discontent and insubordination among the men on the Island, and wholly unjustifiable on the part of the superintendent who, in their opinion, should at all times study to keep up the character and respectability of the Establishment. They do not complain of Mr. Darby in making any suggestions or recommendations which he might consider necessary, but they think that they ought to be made in a proper manner and at a proper time, and not by sweeping charges or personal abuse and invective publicly before the servants and strangers for the time residing on the Island.

No. 6: The superintendent in the case of the "Fulton" has, in the opinion of the commissioners, shown at least great neglect in withholding such information as might be considered necessary to be made known and is usually furnished at the time of the sale of the wreck. The letters (No. 10 and 11) may be referred to on this head. The fact of his making a charge for the board of several passengers of the "Fulton" and receiving in payment therefore money and clothing (as will appear by the documents No. 12 and 13) bears in itself the evidence of a disposition to make money out of those who may be constantly placed under his charge. The Establishment, it is well known, was instituted solely from motives of humanity, and the circumstances of any compensation being required from individuals claiming from necessity its hospitality was considered so disreputable and dangerous to its character that the commissioners did not hesitate in returning the several amounts paid by the individuals alluded to and charging the same against the Establishment.

Halifax, 16th June 1848
Mr. Wallace
J.P. Miller

The documents referred to in this letter follow, but are mixed up with Darby's response to these accusations. Regarding the commissioners' charges, several points stand out. Some of their criticisms are valid, such as their issue with Darby's use of defamatory language around his employees. Two of their points appear to be related to Nesbitt's treatment and testimony. And they again repeat their concerns with the *Fulton*, despite Darby having explained this circumstance many times over. They do mention that some of Darby's affidavits are unsigned, as Nesbitt predicted they would be. Together, these charges formed enough to merit a full investigation of the Sable Island Humane Establishment — or it would have, were Joseph Howe and John Harvey not clearly tired of dealing with this case.

If Darby had indeed falsified the testimonies of some of his employees, then the accounts were clearly not trustworthy. If, on the other hand, they are authentic, then the men must have still had some motive for not providing their signatures. This could have been out of fear of being implicated along with Darby, and losing their positions, or perhaps out of a desire to avoid Darby's short-term wrath with the hopes of his replacement being an easier master. Without further information, the question must be left up in the air.

Three of the testimonies extant in this case are from February of 1848, much earlier than the commissioners' formal list of grievances above. These include accounts from Henry Morash, John Stevens, Jasper Graham, and David Graham. The first testimony from Morash is unsigned, and details Darby's treatment of Nichols while he had scurvy: Nichols was given plenty of food and rest, and received special attention while he recovered. Morash claims Nichols was disobedient, spoke ill of Darby at every opportunity, and didn't do his share of the work.

Darby makes a note elsewhere in his papers that Morash declined to sign this first testimony as he had composed a new one that he was willing to sign. This other document is indeed signed by Henry Morash, and dated to about the same time as the other February testimonies. The first half of the document, which includes the list of rations, was significantly faded and older than the rest of the writing.

> October 5th, one lb bread. Oct. 8th, five lb of oat meal. Oct. 12th, four lb bread and four lb pork. Oct 20th, four lb bread. Oct 28th, four lb bread and four lb pork. November 2nd, four lb pork. November 5th, four lb bread. November 11th, four lb bread. November 17th, six lb of beef. November 14th, six lb of bread.
>
> I certify that I kept this memorandum of provisions spared to Robert Nichols after being ordered by Mr. Darby to give him a full pound of bread and meat per day, with the privilege of as much fish and potatoes as he chose to consume, and if he has not got to that amount in full, it is his own fault, because I would have given it to him by Mr. Darby's order if he wanted it.
>
> As witness, my hand at Sable Island, this 19th day of February 1848.
>
> Henry Morash.
> Sworn to before me this day, 19th of February 1848
> Joseph Darby.

The next testimony is from Darby's brother-in-law, John Stevens, and is signed.

> *I, the undersigned, being called upon by the Superintendent to state what I know concerning a man by the name of Robert Nichol, a hired servant on Sable Island, do solemnly declare, that when the said Nichol first came to the Island, he was very near perishing in assisting to ship the materials of the Afghanistan for want of clothes to keep him warm, which he confessed to me with his own mouth, and I am confident that Mr. Darby immediately afterwards furnished him from his own stores with good and sufficient clothing to keep him comfortable, and enable him to do his duty. That I afterwards heard him complain that it was very hard, that they should have to boil a kettle of tea on the beach to make a nourishing drink, when they were breaking up wood about five miles from home, and had bread and meat with them ready cooked as a bite to enable them to remain until two o'clock, and then quit for the day and come home to their dinners. That Mr. Darby always in speaking about him always spoke favourably of him, that he was a very indifferent boatsman, but still Mr. Darby paid more than ordinary attention to him because he was a mechanic, which I think must have been his only reason for this marked partiality, as he was a very indifferent hand at any work, but blacksmiths work. When that unfortunate ship the Levant was cast away, Nichols showed symptoms of old and inveterate scurvy, and I believe the first that Mr. Darby knew of it, some parts of his flesh was raw. That Mr. Darby immediately removed him out of the boat, and out of the water, and at night he took his horse and rode to the West End 18 miles. And the next morning early, brought him down medicines, oatmeal for gruel, and old linen to bind round his sores, and a pair of soft moleskin under drawers for him to put on, which he gave him. That for two or three days he done but very little work, he would lay on the beach and on two occasions was asleep on the beach. That he would eat and drink and smoke his pipe, and was very saucy and abusive to*

a coloured man in the house, and on the beach. That I have known Mr. Darby to be with five men in a boat working at the wreck of the Milo, that in this work he had every day a bottle of spirits, which he gave entirely to the men and took none himself, with as much bread and meat as they chose to eat, and frequently a kettle of tea, boiled for nourishing drink. That I have frequently been at the West End and have seen how the people lived, that they had the same kind of provisions that I had, and the other people on the Island, which was good and plenty of it, clear cooked, and a clean table laid for them three times a day, with plenty of milk and butter with sometimes liquor, and except that some meat that was sent here was not very good, which I frequently heard him complain of, that we had more fresh meat this year on the Island than I ever knew before, and I have been here altogether about ten years. And that most that is not good cannot be cooked good. And that I have never seen nor heard Mr. Darby strike, kick, or threaten, or use any harsh or bad language to him or to any other man, notwithstanding I think his patience was pretty well tried this season, but he has shown kindness and attention to the wants of every man as far as has been in his power. The service has been unavoidably hard upon all this season, and we have done what we could, and in justice I do not think that there is any thing for a reasonable man to complain of, and I have always thought that Nichols was an artful, designing man. I have always got all my portion in full of whatever liquor came on the Island, I have never got any belonging to the other people. I know Mr. Darby uses none in his family, and I am satisfied that every man has got his full proportion of the liquor sent here for them.

As witness, my hand at Sable Island, this 14th day of February, 1848.

John Stevens.

Sworn to before me, this 14th day of February, 1848.

Joseph Darby, one of HM Justices of the Peace for this District.

This signature from Darby is unique, as he does not invoke this particular role in any other documents. Stevens here provides details that have not been mentioned elsewhere, such as Nichols' specialty as a mechanic, explaining why he was a valuable addition to the island, and why Darby might be keen to keep him even if he was difficult. Stevens gave a detailed account of Darby's kind gestures towards Nichols, down to the moleskin underpants. Considering this document is signed, it is a stronger piece of evidence than some of the other documents provided.

A third testimony is provided in February, this time from Jasper and David Graham. Neither man would sign the document.

> *We the undersigned, being called upon by the superintendent to state what we know about a man by the name of Robert Nichols (a hired servant on Sable Island), having some difference with the said superintendent, do solemnly declare, that we think Mr. Darby treated him with more attention and kindness than he did any other man. That we are well aware that Mr. Darby furnished him with comfortable clothing, and when he first knew of his being afflicted with the scurvy, that he kept him out of the boats and out of the water, and that we think that Mr. Darby furnished him with every necessary that was in his power to furnish, and presented him with some things to try and make sufferings as light as possible. That the work had been very heavy upon us, that at the Levant in particular was most distressingly severe, and yet it seems as if it could hardly be avoided. The labour that eight men did was enough for fifteen or twenty men. That Nichols did not bear an equal part with the others, because he was not able. That some provisions were bad, and that it is impossible to cook bad meat to make it good. About the 14th of August, we the undersigned was cutting wood in the yard, and Mr. Darby was talking to us, that Nichols come behind Mr. Darby, and we believe unperceived by him, and in a rather unbecoming manner, he told Mr. Darby that if he took that horse and put him in harness to work, that he Nichols would have nothing more to do with him, and that he would not go with Jem Clye with the team without he*

sent an other man with them, and he did not go, and Mr. Darby sent Donald Gillis. That Nichols called us to witness what he was saying to Mr. Darby, and to the best of our recollection the worst words that Mr. Darby said to him was to go about his business and not give him any abuse, and he went off cursing and threatening. That we do not believe Mr. Darby knew that any thing was the matter with him when he quit work on the 20th of September, as he always ate very hearty, and drank all the rum he could get. That his statement about going to the East End the second time to look for provisions, we are confident is false, that he had no occasion to do so. We believe he could get provisions whenever he wanted it, and would go for it, and it was frequently carried to him by Henry Morash, who was directed by Mr. Darby to give him what he needed. That there was plenty of salt mackerel, and nice new potatoes all within sixty yards of him, that he could, and we believe he did, make use of as much as he pleased. That he looked fatter and better when he went away than he had done all summer, and that he left two or three pieces of beef in such that he had more than he could eat. And that we have never heard Mr. Darby curse any man, or call them any bad names, or threaten them, or strike, or kick, any man since we have been on the Island, but that he has been with us in boats, and on the beach, at work, where he has given us nourishment, and taken none himself for fear, as he says, that we would not have enough. And we verily believe that but for the constant great care and labour that Mr. Darby's family takes in preparing, making victuals, with milk and butter they provide for the people, their comforts would be much less than what they are, as they often make puddings, pancakes, and short cakes, with also rabbit stews.

These two men, Jasper Graham, and David Graham, have witnessed to me that all the above and within written is strictly true, but they do not like to sign it.

Joseph Darby.

Darby gathered several additional documents and testimonies to support his defence. This included a second document from John Stevens, this time testifying along with Martin Clye. This document is signed by both men, featuring Stevens' signature and an X indicating Clye's mark.

> *We the undersigned, being present during a conversation that passed between the Superintendent and John Nesbitt, which began in the following manner: Nesbitt asked for a barrel of flour on the 2nd Day of May, 1848, and said that the last barrel of flour that he had was bad. Superintendent told him that he was very sorry to hear him continually complaining about his provisions, that he had found fault with his meat, and molasses, and his flour before this, and that he still managed to use a good deal of it. Nesbitt immediately told the superintendent it was a damned lie, he did not complain of the provisions, and if the flour was good it would go twice as far. A good deal of high language followed this in the course of which Nesbitt told the superintendent he did not care a damn for him or his master. Eventually the superintendent told him he would give him no more provisions, but to go to the store himself and take what he wanted, and that he would hear no more complaints from him, and that he went and got the flour himself.*
>
> *As witness, our hands at Sable Island this sixth day of June 1848.*
>
> *John Stevens*
> *Martin Clye, His Mark X*
> *Sworn to before me this 6th day of June 1848*
> *L.O.G Doyle*
> *Notary Public*

This document was not witnessed by Darby, but rather by a notary public.

After this testimony was collected, Darby took it upon himself to pen his final novel-length defence of his own behaviour. He reputed the accusations made against him, including a vast collection of appendices and annexes to support his statements. This document is dated June 28th,

1848.

Province of Nova Scotia
To the Honorables Joseph Howe, James McNab and Hugh Bell, Members of Her Majesty's Executive Council for Nova Scotia
The Memorial of Joseph Darby, Superintendent of Sable Island
Most respectfully sheweth that your memorialist having left the Island and proceeded to Halifax in obedience to a letter of the commissioners of the first of one instant - for the purpose as well of giving information regarding the management and condition of the Island - as of answering certain charges made against him by the commission and others. And your memorialist having been favoured with the written statement of the commissioners under oath the 16th. Instant, wherein these charges are embodied, and these charges being in the opinion of your memorialist capable of easy explanation - your memorialist begs leave to call the attention of your Honours, to whom he understands these matters have been referred to the following statements and observations explanatory of the charges and insinuations made against him and which he feels will be entirely unmoved by an impartial investigation.
The first in order is a change against the superintendent of unjustifiable conduct in the treatment of R.C. Nichols a servant of the Establishment. This man arrived on the Island in the month of April 1847. He was at that time in want of proper clothing to enable him to withstand the severity of the weather and to fit him for his duties. The superintendent at once furnished him with good and sufficient clothing out of his own private stores. The conduct of Nichols up to the 14th of August last was in general satisfactory - as far as it came under the observation of the superintendent. He was a good Blacksmith - tho' but seldom called upon to exercise his trade. But in other respects he was quite an ordinary hand and by no means the useful man some persons on the Island have been endeavouring to represent him. The superintendent paid more than usual attention to this man, simply because he was a mechanic and superintendent wished to encourage him to remain

upon the Island. At the time of the wreck of the Levant early in August last, this man showed symptoms of old scurvy and the superintendent as soon as his attention was called to the fact had him at once removed from the boats and from the water, and on the next day went himself to the West End Establishment, about 18 miles from the wreck and procured medicines, oatmeal, linen, moleskin drawers and other necessaries for him with which he at once returned. Nichols remained idle on the beach with the Superintendent's permission every day during their stay at the wreck, doing occasionally a little service in holding the horses or driving the team; feasting every day as well as the next who were hard at work, and returning every evening with the rest of the party to the East End Establishment a short distance from the wreck, where they all used to sleep and where they got their breakfast, dinner and supper. All this time Nichols ate and drank as heartily as any of the others. There was no liquor with them at this time.

On the 17th of August while at headquarters and during the prepping season of hay-making. Nichols was ordered by the superintendent to go with the team, then in the yard, to haul grass from the marsh about four miles off, and to assist in loading and driving; Nichols' horse being in the team superintendent thought it desirable that he should be with the animal as it had not been broken in. Nichols refused to go unless the superintendent would send some other man than James Clye, who was then in charge of the team. He gave no reason for not wishing to go with Clye. He used a good deal of abusive language to the superintendent on this occasion and refused most positively to obey his orders. The two Grahams who were in the yard at the time heard and saw all that passed – indeed Nichols himself called their attention to it – superintendent laid his hand gently on his shoulders and begged him to be quick and so to some other work. He went away cursing and threatening to all which the Superintendent at that time paid no further attention. Another man, Donald Gillis, was sent with the team in his place and Nichols went to other work about the premises. From this time to the third of September, Nichols was working at the hay under the direction of Henry Morash. On this day, the Superintendent, when at the barn, directed Morash to send out a man from the barn to pitch the hay into the loft. Nichols, who was in the barn at the time, said in a tone sufficiently loud for Superintendent to hear, "Fork it up yourself". Superintendent pretended not to hear this and went away without making any observation about it.

On Sunday, September 19*th*, Superintendent had occasion about half past seven in the morning to call up the people, as usual, to bring their turn of water for the house. Nichols, on being called, answered from his room upstairs "Go to Hell". Superintendent did not notice this insult, thinking it better to let him suppose that he hadn't heard it.

From this period to the 30*th* of September, Nichols was occupied with Morash about the hay and fishing. On this day, Superintendent ordered him to assist in cutting and bringing sods for banking the fireplace in the oil house. This he refused to do in the most positive manner, using a great deal of saucy and abusive language. He said he was not able to go, but did not allege any reason. Superintendent thought that Nichols had by this time got quite cured of his scurvy, as he had returned to work, ate heartily, drank more liquor than the others, and had made no complaints to the Superintendent since the early part of August. The conduct of Nichols on this occasion was such as could not well be passed over without severe consequence or punishment, as it tended to the immediate subversion of the authority and respect with which the Superintendent should at all times be inverted. All this took place in the yard before the house where Nichols and the other men lodged and some time before breakfast that morning. Superintendent left Nichols in the yard. He was not at breakfast that morning. In the course of the day it was found that he had either gone away or concealed himself. Neither the Superintendent nor others knew or could imagine what had become of him.

This part of the story picks up at the same part where the remaining journal from this year begins. Nichols' disappearance is noted by the superintendent.

> As soon as his desertion was discovered, diligent search was at once made for him, and particularly on board Captain Crowell's vessel the Victoria when at the Island. In the course of the day, Superintendent seized Nichols' clothes and other property and took charge of them as forfeited under the laws and regulations of the Island made for disobedience of orders and absence without leave.
>
> Superintendent saw nothing more of Nichols till the 4th of October when he was brought to headquarters by John Stephens from the foot of the lake. Stevens saying that Nesbitt had, the day before, brought him to the lake and had refused to allow him to remain any longer at the East End Establishment.
>
> From this period, the Superintendent treated Nichols as a person guilty of insubordination and put him upon the allowance considered proper under the Island regulations, as a castaway or idle person. The Superintendent consulted with Henry Morash as the most suitable diet for a person in his condition and ordered Morash to give him a pound of bread or bread stuffs and pound of beef per day, with as much potatoes and fish as he chose to make use of, of which there was abundance within his reach. Any further supply of such things as milk, oatmeal, rabbits, etc. he could have had whenever he chose, and may have had them for all that Superintendent knows to the contrary. Once or twice, Superintendent inquired of Morash whether Nichols was getting enough and told Morash to take care that he was well supplied. This treatment of Nichols, though it has since been considered severe and by the Commissioners, reported as unjustifiable, was imperatively called for under the circumstances, richly deserved by Nichols, and absolutely necessary in order to enforce discipline and maintain the authority of the Superintendent. Indeed, the most rigid and stern exercise of such authority may at times be

demanded to preserve the very existence, well being, and efficiency of the whole establishment. It was painful to the Superintendent to be obliged in this instance to resort to this extreme exercise of this authority. He considered this mode of dealing with him preferable to the harsher punishment of personal restraint or confinement. The Superintendent was not made aware of any suffering of Nichols or of any extraordinary inconvenience experienced by him in consequence of this treatment. He gave no further trouble. On the 18th November, the Schooner Daring *arrived. Nichols went on board after without the Superintendent's knowledge or permission and without the knowledge or permission of the Captain of the Schooner, and arrived at Halifax. His clothes and other things seized in the manner already stated, having been put onboard, directed to the Commissioners as soon as it was discovered that Nichols had left.*

This description of events is far more specific than what Darby wrote in the journals. In the November entry, he wrote simply that Nichols left on the *Daring* and that his things were sent along to the commissioners. Only here does Darby elaborate that Nichols went on board secretly, and specify that his belongings were sent along afterwards. These stories do more or less line up.

Darby specifically addressed points within Nichols' testimony that he disagreed with. He pointed out that there was no reason for Nichols to have been out on the road between stations for 36 hours as he claimed, as the house at the foot of the lake was only nine miles from headquarters. Darby also questioned the validity of Nesbitt's testimonies. "Nesbitt could know nothing of what had taken place at headquarters except what Nichols told him," Darby pointed out. "Nesbitt speaks of three visits made to the East End by Nichols, while Nichols himself mentions only two." Darby claimed that there was no merit to any of the stories about Nichols being deprived of food. "When Nichols went away from the island, he looked fat and well and left some pieces of the best beef on the island which he could not consume."

Interestingly, Darby refers to a letter sent to him by the

superintendents in February following Nichols' departure from the island. "A copy of Nichols' letter was forwarded to the superintendent with a letter from the Commissioners," he wrote, "wherein they state that this man 'being inclined to give all the trouble he possibly could', and as he might be called before a committee of the House of Assembly, they requested the superintendent to reply as fully as he could, and to provide all the evidence on the subject in his power to procure." After receiving this letter of warning, Darby claimed to have composed a defence and sent it along to Halifax.

In his final defence, Darby explained why an 11 year old boy was on the payroll as a cook. "The duty itself is in general disagreeable to men who seldom give satisfaction," Darby said in explanation as to why nobody else wanted the job. "The cooking, when strangers were employed, had usually been done in a slovenly and careless manner, and one man in particular by the name of Bellows had been detected in using water from a ditch or mud puddle near at hand to make soup with." The accusation of putting the boy on payroll under a false name was explained by the fact that the boy's full name was Thomas Fitzgerald Uniacke Darby, and that only his first two names had appeared on the paperwork. Though the boy was young, Darby said that he was "assisted by his mother and three sisters, with the occasional aid of a hired female and without further expense to the Establishment." The women of Darby's family were certainly taking on a great deal of work around the island, but weren't eligible to be paid for their services. The hiring Thomas Fitzgerald appeared to be a loophole to this fact. Darby pointed out the great strain that the labour put on his family, especially during the event of a shipwreck when more people needed to be fed. "In the commencement of 1847, the Superintendent's family have baked bread to the extent of 90 pounds a day, besides other work. Baking has usually to be done for 15 or 16 persons, and sometimes for the whole Establishment." He went on to add that his family continued to bear this burden since the boy had been dismissed from his post, without remuneration or another person sent to serve as cook.

Another accusation was that Darby was selling liquor to the people of the island. The people were each allotted a portion of alcohol, so if

Darby had been selling it to them, he was certainly defrauding them in the process. But Darby explained that he and his sons did not consume their shares of the alcohol, and would simply offer their shares for sale to the people if they desired more than what they were allotted.

After providing his defences against sundry other charges, Darby concluded his report.

> *Your memorialist having thus gone through the various charges made against him, and having endeavoured to answer them in, he trusts, no unkind spirit, he would in conclusion say that your memorialist has been in the service of this Establishment since the year 1807. That he has resided on the Island since 1830. And during all that long period, he believes, he has been faithful to the best interests of the Establishment. An immense quantity of property has been saved, to say nothing of six hundred lives preserved since 1830. The report of Captain Townshend shows the vast improvements that have been made since the Superintendent has been in charge, and the creditable state of the Establishment at this moment. Your memorialist has at different times received from crowned heads valuable marks of their distinguished consideration.*
>
> *Your memorialist appeals to those who have been longest on the Island to retain his character from imputations of violence or excess in the exercise of his authority. Those who have known him best and who have themselves been the most faithful servants can testify as to the correctness of assertions made by parties who, having themselves no character to lose, are careless of the reputation of others.*
>
> *The Commissioners themselves have acknowledged the general character and conduct of your memorialist have been commendable and praise-worthy, and your memorialist can only say that if in his zeal to benefit the Establishment and to preserve order, he has either in the case of Nichols or at any other time been guilty of excess or gone beyond the bounds of prudence appropriately, the errors of the part of such they shall be considered will serve as beacons to light his pathway for the future.*

> *Your memorialist trusts his statements will meet with a candid and unpremeditated consideration, and he hopes that he may not fall a sacrifice to the arts of the designing, the reckless, or the depraved.*
>
> *And as in duty bound, your memorialist will ever pray etc.*
> *Joseph Darby*
> *Superintendent, Sable Island*
> *Halifax, June 28th, 1848*

Following this significant document's production, Darby remained in Halifax for further discussions. He returned to Sable Island in July, and continued his correspondence with Joseph Howe in an effort to maintain his job, or at the very least, his reputation.

The case concluded with a letter to Darby from William Howe, which included the results of the court's decision in the case. He is sympathetic to Darby, but expresses an inability to do anything for him until the government changes over.

> *Halifax, Nov 1st 1848*
> *My dear sir,*
> *I received your letter of September 26th and am availing myself of the departure of the Daring to unite a few lines. I was desirous to leave written you before and given you some notice of the intentions of the government. But I never could discover an opportunity. Tho' I have asked the Commissioners several times, I annex you an abstract of the report made by the gentleman of the council to the executive after the investigation. I hardly knew whether I ought to let you know so much about it but upon reflection I thought it better that you should know the worst. When you leave to read it you will perceive that they have taken a much more unfavourable view of the matter than could have been expected. I asked for the favour of perusing the draft of the report and endeavoured my strong remonstrance, to induce the gentlemen of the council to make it less harsh, but I soon perceived that all efforts were useless.*

You will perceive that in making the accompanying abstract I have frequently quoted the <u>very words</u> of the report. I have given a correct outline of the report and you will have no difficulty in forming an idea of its tenor. With such a report before His Excellency you cannot of course wonder at the result. You see that even where you are seemingly acquitted there is some damning clause added which spoils everything. Of course you will after carefully reading which I send be better able to decide upon the propriety or advantage of further stirring in the matter, as to being re-instated that is out of the question. You must wait for a change of administration. The House of Assembly being all composed of the same materials would of course take the same view of the matter as the council. It is useless to indulge in hope of a reunion at this junction of affairs.

I waited on the Provincial Secretary as you desired but was not encouraged to entertain any hope of obtaining any of your wishes. He said if you wished, you possibly might get a lighthouse or something of that sort but he did not know what else could be done. He said that if you thought the council had done you injustice you might stir the matter in the House of Assembly But that it rested with you whether the matter should have any publicity. The matter should not be mentioned if you wished and the papers might lie in the holes of his office desk undisturbed.

Judge Sawers desires to join me in kind regards and sympathy for what has happened, but begs to say that having lost his office of Recorder and having no official access to Government House he could not if he wished be of the slightest service to you just now. I have sent you journals.

I should be happy to further your interests in any way but do not know just now what can be done, but submit, I am told you are expected here shortly. In the mean time believe me. Yours very truly

William Howe

Howe appeared to be truly sympathetic to Darby's cause, viewing him as yet another casualty of the changing political scene in Nova Scotia. As Darby did not continue the fight, it seems likely that he wished to avoid further publicity. He would only go on to seek a pension from the government after several years.

The summary of the court findings sent by William Howe include a list of the concise charges against Darby, and their findings relating to each.

<u>Charges against the Superintendent</u>
1st: General severity, harshness, and violence of manner towards the people on the island.
2nd: Nichols' treatment.
3rd: Etter's treatment.
4th: Disrespect to Commissioners.
5th: Selling liquor.
6th: Entering his son Thomas FW Darby, a lad, on the articles.
7th: Charging wrecked passengers for cooking, etc.
8th: Supplying his son's vessels with provisions, etc.
9th: Taking advantage of his position to promote the interest of his family with reference to "Lady Echo" and "Fulton".

Making fair allowance for the difficulties of the Superintendent's position, and freely acknowledging that many imputations injurious to his character were wholly unfounded, still the committee are reluctantly compelled to state, that the "main charges" have been fully proved, and that there is too much reason to believe that "undue advantage has been taken of his position for the profit of his family".

Each of the charges listed above were addressed with the following resolutions.

1st: The committee acquit Superintendent of habitual tyranny, harshness and inhumanity, but still, say, that from "habits *of supreme command he has fallen into "a <u>morbid irritability</u> which cannot brook opposition, criticism or remonstrance". This is evidenced by the correspondence and log. The treatment of Nichols may account for the bitter feelings of resentment some of the subordinates entertain. This frame of mind is <u>not desirable</u> in a person entrusted with such a command. It is unfortunate when the men on the Island "boldly impeach the integrity or humanity of Superintendent and he again impeaches the Commissioners and considers him, such a disorganized community is not creditable to the Province, and in periods of peril might be injurious".*

2nd: Granted that the Island care gave to Superintendent the power exercised in the care of Nichols. Yet Nichols had worked some time with credit and was so useful that Superintendent was proposing a partnership with him at Halifax. This treatment followed the discovery of his writing to the Commissioners, while sick and irritated with scurvy he was subjected to the severest penalties of the Island care, kept apart for 7 weeks without means of cooking and without a clean shirt.

3rd: Etter's case. This involves three parties, his guardians, the Commissioners, and Superintendent. Report describes Etter as, "a person of some property unvisited and uncared for, the drudge and the butt of the Island, squalid and half clad, beaten and taunted till every attribute of manhood and every dawn of intellect were vanished and clouded by the monotonous degradation of an existence." The Commissioners not free from blame. The £15 paid by Etter's friends went into the pocket of the Superintendent while Etter was maintained at the expense of the public, and must have cost in - years at - a year at least £[blank]. The Commissioners should have broken up the arrangement tho not responsible for its origin. The superintendent may have acted towards Etter on the exploded notion of coercion etc being "the only restorative of a disordered intellect", yet even this would hardly justify "the scene sketched by Jackson with much loathsome accuracy".

4th: This charge, disrespect to Commissioners, proved by correspondence and log. The Superintendent should have resigned if dissatisfied with the Commissioners and not have shown an example of insubordination to those under him and of disrespect to his superiors.

5th: Selling liquor. Superintendent has not denied that he did so till 1845. When he submitted "with a bad grace if at all", the desire to sell being a source of irritation between him and commissioners up to this time. Morash and elect say that liquor could be had at any time since 1846 by the one in favor and who chose to pay. Without deciding whether his or their statements is the correct one taking the admitted facts, the conclusion is, that as in other cases, "a desire to secure pecuniary profit" seems to have been indulged in "to the total disregard of the relative position of the superintendent and those around him". If it would be discreditable to a Captain of a man of war to sell grog, equally so to a person in a command like that of Superintendent, and being a justice of the peace he should have known better.

6th: This charge is frankly admitted. Acting as superintendent did in this case and "thereby committing a fraud for his own advantage and properly deceiving the Commissioners, are acts that however palliated or explained admit of no excuse". Admitting what Superintendent says, yet "the false entry and the deception remain" as evidence among other things, to lead to the conclusion, that "a desire for gain", totally at variance with the spirit that should be diffused through an Establishment devoted to humanity was too strong to be controlled and prepare the mind to examine the evidence bearing in the two last and by far the most important charges.

7th: Money was taken from wrecked passengers for cooking

etc. admit that the amount was small and that these persons could afford it, still if such thing were done in one instance, there is no security that it had not been done before or that it would not be repeated. As every inmate of the family was supposed at the public expense any little service, should have been given cheerfully and gratis. The character of the Establishment might otherwise be compromised.

8th: The evidence on this charge is a vague and inconclusive, and it is fair to state that several injurious inferences and imputations unfairly drawn were disproved by unexceptionable testimony, unfairly explained, but committee deems it unfortunate that deep seated suspicions should rest on the minds of most of the witnesses, and however engendered are to be deplored.

9th. The Fulton *and* Lady Echo. *"The Committees have given to all the circumstances bearing in this matter a great deal of anxious consideration." In the preservation of wrecked property various interests are involved. The public have a right to fair competition, and the government have a direct interest in this honourable rivalry. There can be no fair competition if the Superintendent and those possessing superior means of information are allowed to purchase. The Lady Echo was stranded in 1846 in September. She was nearly new, of about 40 tons. Superintendent represents as follows, "She is a wreck" etc etc see letter. With such an account there were of course no bidders. Commissioners buy her for 40% in 16th Nov. She is <u>nominally</u> sold to Mr Deblois, but really became the property of J.H. Darby. Of this purchase Superintendent says he knew nothing till the Spring. This the committee "do not believe". The Daring was there October 27th, affording an opportunity to tell him and consult etc etc. The Daring visited the Island again in January and February after the sale. The vessel being registered in J.E. Darby's name, in December 29th yet Superintendent says that he did not know that his son had any interest in her. Yet some, being gave her an* *increased value in his eye, before the sale she is almost worthless, after the sale "all the Island force is exerted to haul her up". Much labor is bestowed on her in the fall of 1846. In the spring all the disposable force and complaints employed, nothing was paid to the Province for this labor, blocks, rigging, etc. were said to have been furnished. The difference of what she sold for and what she would have sold at, went not into the treasury but into the pocket of Superintendent's son. The superior advantage of information possessed by Superintendent and family would restrain competition and dissatisfaction would naturally arise among the men in the Island by being obliged to work for the family.*

The Fulton, *an American Schooner of beautiful model and copper fastened with a cargo of 500 quintals of dry fish and 550 barrels of pickled fish and 2 casks of copper, came on shore on NW point in February, and was in no danger of drifting off. The Superintendent in his letter reports etc etc see letter. With such a description it is not astonishing that she sold for £25, the fish afterwards sold for £[blank] and the copper for £65. The vessel is now sound and requires little outlay to get her off. Even if the son had derived no advantage from this yet it is far from creditable. The Commissioners say to Superintendent that he is guilty of neglect in withholding full information. The Commissioners are to blame too in not advertising etc. but they derived no advantage either before or after the sale. If this transaction stood alone it could not be looked at without great regret, but coupled with the other things, it shows a desire to grasp at personal advantage by unfair means, and the Government cannot pass it over with credit to themselves or a due regard to the intent of the public.*

The case was closed. Both Darby and the commissioners were out of a job; however, the commissioners were wealthy men who had other businesses to fall back on. Darby was put in the difficult position of being without a job, and in possession of a damaged reputation.

He and his family returned to Halifax. We find a bittersweet account of those last island days in the journal of his replacement, M.D.

McKenna.

> *1848, Wednesday, 8th Nov.*
> *At 7 AM made the West End of the Island. At 8 came to anchor abreast of the Flag Staff. The boat came off and reported the sea too high for us to hand safely, the boat went on shore with a few of our things, returned and took us all on shore. On landing met Mr. Joseph Darby on the beach who stated his intentions of going off with his family on the* Daring.
> *The wind blowing fresh from NW and a heavy sea on shore, the* Daring *weighed anchor and stood to sea. In the course of the day, took a last ramble with Mr. Darby through the premises. 4 PM, the* Daring *10 miles North of the Island under easy sails.*
> *This day ends with strong NW winds and clear weather.*
> *Thursday, 9th Nov.*
> *Begins with fresh NW winds, and clear weather. 8 AM, more moderate. The* Daring *came to anchor abreast of the Flag Staff, and all hands employed landing and taking on board at the same time. Noon calm. 4 PM all our furniture landed and Mr. Darby's furniture, a lot of berries, and some wrecked materials, also the crew of the Spanish Schooner* Bella Maria, *all on board. Mr. And Mrs. Darby, three daughters, one son, and William Etter embark. 5 PM, the* Daring *underway for Halifax. Hauled up the boat and made all secure.*
> *Ends with strong gales from the southward and heavy rain.*

And so, as a storm broke over the Atlantic, Darby's life on Sable Island ended.

Chapter Five

Darby's Retirement

Some years after his departure from Sable Island, Darby wrote a letter to the latest lieutenant governor to ask for a pension which he was promised after his dismissal. In this final correspondence from Darby himself, we see a proud man who is aware of his life's many achievements, and knows keenly what services he provided to the province. As predicted by William Howe's letter years earlier, there had been a change in government, and perhaps Darby was able to receive a more favourable response this time.

> *Excellency Major General Sir John Gaspard LeMarchant, Knight, Knight Commander of the order of St Ferdinand and of Charles the third of Spain, Lieutenant Governor and Commander in Chief in and over Her Majesty's Province of Nova Scotia and its Dependencies, etc etc.*
>
> *The humble petition of the undersigned sheweth, that your petitioner was connected with Sable Island and its affairs for a period of over forty two years. That the establishment was formed in 1802 and that his father was the first man that conveyed the supplies to the Island in his own vessel, which he continued to do for a number of years.*

> *That in 1807, your petitioner, then a youth, was sent to the Island by his father to assist the Superintendent where he remained until 1811. That he subsequently piloted the* Shannon Frigate, Captain Broke, *and conducted her safe to Sable Island and brought away from thence the Captain, Officers, Crew, and prisoners of H.M. Ship* Barbados, *wrecked there with sixty three thousand dollars, and captured a most troublesome privateer called the Wily Reynard.*
>
> *That in 1814, your petitioner joined his father in the purchase of a smart Schooner named the* Two Brothers *for the service of Sable Island, of which he was the Master, and sailed under a protection or convention signed by the American Government and the Government of Nova Scotia against all public...*

The letter is cut off, a middle page gone missing. Darby later continues:

> *...at the course pursued towards him and the imputations affecting his character as well as being very seriously injured by being cast adrift without any notice and thereby deprived of the means of maintaining his family; he appealed to the House of Assembly, praying them to investigate the charges against him, and do your petitioner that justice to which he felt himself entitled.*
>
> *And your petitioner further sheweth that the paper writing hereunto annexed marked A is a true copy of the report made to the House by the Committee, to whom the petition of your petitioner was referred to which your petitioner craves leave to solicit your Excellency's particular attention.*
>
> *And your petitioner further sheweth unto Your Excellency that he has in his possession numerous letters and certificates in his favour from the leading merchants of the city and others of unquestionable respectability, ready to be produced in his behalf should Your Excellency desire their production.*
>
> *And your petitioner lastly sheweth unto Your Excellency,*

DARBY'S RETIREMENT

that no action has since been taken by the Honourable the House of Assembly on the report, and that your petitioner has never received any portion of the annual pension recommended to be paid him in the said report.

Your petitioner therefore humbly prays that your Excellency would be pleased to take the circumstances of his case into consideration and reappoint him to the situation of Superintendent of Sable Island, from which he was dismissed without adequate grounds; and grant your petitioner such other relief in the premises as to Your Excellency may seem meet and justice may require

And your petition, as in duty bound, will ever pray,
Joseph Darby.

Tracing Darby's story after leaving Sable Island is challenging. He appears to have settled in Halifax Ward 5, where the 1851 Census lists him as the head of household. There were three other names listed as household heads under his; G. Blair, M. McKinlay, and another illegible. There were four families living between the two houses on the property. These were all younger families; only two people on the census were listed as above the age of 50 — Darby was about 63 years old at the time, and his wife could have been the other senior in the residence. The household had three children (one boy, two girls) under 10 years old, a boy and a girl between 10-20 years old, a man and a woman in their twenties, a man and woman in their thirties, and a man and two women in their forties. It is difficult to determine what led to this communal living situation, but it is possible that renting to these three younger families was an income stream for the elderly Darbys.

The 1861 Census suggests this situation continues. Joseph Darby is listed as the only head of household at this time, with nine people living with him: five males and four females. Among them was a baby girl, born in the year before the Census. Darby didn't provide any information for the other census categories including disabilities and the ability to read or write among the household members. From the little information provided this year, it appears that the Darbys were still cohabiting with younger families.

He didn't make many waves after departing from the island, with the exception of a talk given to Halifax's Athenaeum Society in 1858. This talk, along with a lecture by J. Bernard Gilpin and a poem by Joseph Howe both on the subject of Sable Island, was preserved in a publication from the same year. Darby's talk was titled "A Description of the Shipwreck of the American Schooner *Arno*, Lost on the Island September 19, 1846", and he is credited as *Joseph Darby, Esq., Superintendent of the Island*. It seems that despite the bad press that surrounded Darby's departure, there was no *damnatio memorae* regarding his service to the island.

Wreck of the Schooner Arno by Joseph Darby, Esq.

Mr. President, Ladies and Gentlemen, — Having been invited here this evening to give some explanatory statements of particular events that occurred on Sable Island during my Superintendence of that Establishment, and not previously having had sufficient notice to refresh my memory by reflecting back to the occurrences as they happened, I fear that my statements, although substantially correct in the outline, may have lost through failure of memory a great many incidents worthy of notice, and fully and legitimately connected with them. Hoping that you will make allowance for the lapse of time and the omissions that may have thus occurred, I will, at the request of the President, make some comments on the circumstances that occurred on the 19th and 20th of September, 1846, as in their nature they are partly mixed and blended together.

On the 19th of September, 1846, the Government Schr. Daring, commanded by my oldest son, came to the Island for the purpose of conveying to Halifax the crew and materials of the wreck of the ship Detroit, *lately stranded there with her crew and passengers; also, the crew of the schooner* Lady Echo *lately stranded there. We got the Schooner down the North side to the wreck of* Detroit, *about ten miles to the Eastward of Head-quarters, and* *commenced shipping her materials, and the work went on with vigour and alacrity. The day was moderate, with light airs of wind from the Eastward. It was a clear and cloudless day, but it had a certain dull and leaden appearance about it, that seemed to portend a gathering of the elements together, as if for strife. The sea ran high although there was no wind, and gave us a good deal of trouble, by often filling our loaded boats in crossing the bars, where it often broke very bad, and rolled along the shore with a groaning, uneasy and very troubled sound. After the sun passed the Meridian, the gloom and dulness seemed to increase, the sea rose higher although but little wind, and the moaning sound of the waters as they broke along the strand seemed to give strong indications of a coming storm. Our work proceeded successfully, notwithstanding the difficulties we had to content with; — the property was all shipped, the vessel loaded and ready for sea, and at half an hour after sunset she got under weigh, with our boat and boat's crew to be towed up to head quarters and landed there. The wind was now a fresh breeze from East. I got on my horse to keep abreast of the vessel, which I did until dark. I had ten miles to go to the landing place, I drove to that point as fast as I could, and then rushed on to the beach to watch the arrival of my boat. It was now very dark, with a fresh breeze, and the sea rising very fast. The whole ocean appeared to be a phosphoretic blaze of light; and the very minute marine animalculae seemed each one to have its own light, and to increase the natural phenomena. I soon observed our boat coming directly towards me: I jumped off my horse, and as I always rode with six fathoms of light line on my horse's neck, one end I fastened there, and the other end I tied to my leg. I was then able to assist my people in the boat without loosing my horse, as she filled and turned over just as she got within my reach. The people reported that the schooner hauled off to sea the moment that the boat left her. We hauled up and secured our boat for an approaching gale, then went to the house, changed our wet clothes, got supper, and set a watch. At midnight the watch reported heavy gale of wind from E.N.E.; at four o'clock the morning of the*

20th, a most terrific gale of wind with rain from the N.E.; and at daylight the gale to be still increasing, and the wind veering to the N.N.E. All hands out. The hull of the schooner Lady Echo, *that had been wrecked near the landing, could be seen from the lookout house to be floating and knocking about on the beach, and we had to crawl on our hands and knees across the Island to where her cargo of barrels of mackerel was piled up, — the wind being so violent we could not proceed against it in an upright position. We found the cargo in danger of being smashed to pieces by the sea, and we commenced parbuckling it up the bank to a place of comparative safety, and we were so occupied until about noon; and it was this circumstance that brought us all out there in that terrific gale, as if Providence directed that we should all be out and all together so as to be the better prepared for what was going to follow. All of a sudden, we saw an object off the North side dead to windward which we first thought was a large bird, but shortly after discovered that it was a sail distant five or six miles, and that she was running down right before this tremendous gale dead on a lee-shore. We could work no more at the barrels. Our eyes were strained in the direction of the object that appeared to be running to inevitable destruction. My first impression was that it was the schooner* Daring *which had left the Island the evening before, and that they had met with some disaster so as to disable the vessel in the gale, and were going to run her on shore before night to save their lives.*

We could now see that she was a schooner with a close-reefed mainsail set, steering directly for our flag-staff. I was convinced that it was my son, who with two of his sisters on board, and a great number of other passengers, were taking this method to preserve their lives. I fell on my knees and prayed most earnestly and devoutly to the Almighty to have mercy on them, as I did not doubt but they were praying too, and that to a God who they were taught to believe was a hearer of prayer. The sea was breaking everywhere off the North side as far as the eye could see, and it appeared almost incredible that any vessel could live to come so great a distance through such mountains of broken water. I got a rope prepared, to assist in preserving the people's lives should the vessel be able to reach the beach through the roaring and boiling mountains of water that surrounded her. When she approached within three miles of the land she appeared to be in the heaviest breakers, and we could plainly perceive mountain waves on each side of her that would raise their curled heads as high as the tops of her masts and pitch over and fall with the weight of hundreds of tons, either of which would have been sufficient to have smashed that frail bark to atoms; but, miraculous as it may appear, not one of them touched her. No — that heaven-favored vessel was under the protection of an Omnipotent God, and guided by a Master-hand, and neither winds nor waves were permitted to destroy the souls on board. At one moment you could just perceive the heads of her masts between the mountains of waters that were smashing and breaking to pieces all around, but not permitted to hurt her; at the next moment you would see her on the top of a tremendous wave which appeared like certain destruction to her; at another, you would see a mountainous sea rising up before her and breaking all to fragments in her path, but when she arrived at the spot the surface was smooth as glass. When she arrived within one mile of the shore she had to pass over what we call the Outer Bar, where every sea broke from the bottom, and our greatest anxiety for the safety of the vessel was at this point. The sea was there breaking with tremendous violence, but that heaven-favored bark passed through untouched, — the sea became smooth before her, and she left a shining track behind. Now, here was the miracle. I looked on this with wonder, awe and admiration, and not without hope. When she approached a little nearer, I could see one man lashed at the helm and two men forward lashed by each of the fore-shrouds, and by each man a large cask standing on end. We could also see that the two men were making great exertions with their arms, as if throwing something up in the wind. The vessel had now passed the most dangerous place, and her safety seemed certain, — I could breathe much freer than I had done for some minutes. Another half-mile brought her to the beach, and her bow struck the sand. From this spot to the high bank was about fifty or sixty yards over a flat beach, which was always dry except in heavy gales, but was now covered over with water. A number of heavy seas would roll together over the beach, and then recede, leaving it dry. Over this space myself and the men were extended with a rope leading from the bank down to the vessel's bow, on which we held to keep the sea from washing us away; and when the great body of water receded, we could approach as near as the jib-boom end, from which, one by one, the crew lowered themselves by a rope into our arms, and we passed them in safety to the bank. They were all entire strangers. The captain was a praying man, and indeed a clever man; his first act after getting on shore was to go aside with me and return thanks to his Maker for their miraculous preservation.

He then told me his story. The Schooner was the Arno, *Capt. Higgins, with twelve men, from the Quero Bank, where they had been fishing. They left the Bank at the commencement of the gale. He had lost all his head sails when at daylight this morning he made the land dead under his lee, with the gale blowing right on shore. The vessel having no head-sail, he could do nothing with her on a wind. He let go his anchor in twenty fathoms of water, payed out three hundred fathoms of hemp cable, and brought the vessel head to wind. In that tremendous sea he held on until noon, when, seeing no prospect of the gale abating, he cut his cable and put the vessel before the wind, preferring to run her on shore before night to riding there and foundering at her anchor. He lashed himself to the helm, sent all his men below but two, and nailed up the cabin-doors. He had two large casks placed near the fore-shrouds and lashed there. He then directed his two best men to station themselves there and lash themselves firmly to the casks, which were partly filled with blubber and oil from the fish. They had each a wooden ladle of about two feet long, and with those ladles they dipped up the blubber and oil and threw it up in the air as high as they could. The great violence of the wind carried it far to leeward, and, spreading over the water, made its surface smooth before her and left a shining path behind; and although the sea would rise very high, yet the top of it was smooth, and never broke where the oil was. It was raging, pitching and breaking close to her on each side, but not a barrel of water fell upon her deck the whole distance. The vessel was so old and tender that she went all to pieces in a very short time after the crew, with their clothing and provisions, were saved.*

Thus was preserved in a most miraculous manner this crew of good men; and although the finger of God was seen and felt in this circumstance, yet it was brought about by natural means. I had often heard of oil smoothing the face of turbid waters, but I could hardly have believed that under the present circumstances, — even had I known that the oil was used as the means to produce such an effect, — that it would have been possible to subdue and smoothen so very rough and boisterous a surface.

A few years later, Joseph Darby's life came quietly to an end in Halifax. His obituary appeared in a few newspapers at the end of April, 1863. The longest passage came in the Acadian Recorder on April 25th.

Suddenly, this morning, Joseph Darby, Esq., aged 76 years. Funeral from his late residence, No. 62. Brunswick Street, on Monday, at 3 o'clock. Friends and acquaintances are respectfully requested to attend without further notice.

Darby's final residence was in a long-gone building on Brunswick street, which has since been renumbered. He would have had a view of Citadel Hill and the Halifax Town Clock from his window. He went on to be buried in Camp Hill Cemetery, the final resting place for so many of Nova Scotia's important early figures.

Joseph Darby's story has remained murky for over one hundred and fifty years. He is written in the history of Sable Island as a rogue, or a cruel man, or a villain. These descriptors go along well with the image of Darby that the commissioners and unhappy employees of Sable Island wished to paint at the end of his career. But in his long career with the Sable

Island Humane Establishment, from working on his father's supply ship to running the entire island in the company of his beloved sons, Joseph Darby encountered so many adventures and obstacles that it is difficult to ascribe a single moniker to him, besides this: a man of Sable Island.

Acknowledgements

This book was a labour of love inspired by the transcription work that I did for the Friends of Sable Island Society. I give them full credit for introducing me to Darby and the world of Sable Island, and thank them for the many opportunities they've given me to further my curiosity about this weird and wonderful little island. In particular I'd like to thank April Hennigar and Glenn Bartlett for their support, encouragement, and trust.

The Nova Scotia Archives are responsible for housing and protecting nearly all of the historical documents that were consulted for this book. They also provided me with a high-quality copy of Darby's original map, which I was able to convert to greyscale for the purpose of including sections of it in this book. If you're interested in Sable Island's history, I highly recommend checking out their collection, starting with their online archive Footprints in the Sand.

As always I'd like to thank my family for their support of my writing career. I began writing this book a month after dropping out of my PhD program and moving back to Canada, and it wouldn't have been possible without my parents giving me the time and space in their home to change careers in my own stubborn and non-linear way.

Finally, I'd like to thank my friend and colleague Alexander Duguay for encouraging me to put life back into this manuscript after I had originally left it for dead. Your beautiful design skills take my words to the next level and made this a real Book (with a capital B).

Author Bio

R.E. WILSON is an academic-turned-writer based in Halifax, Nova Scotia. She holds an MA in Classics and an MA in English from Memorial University and Acadia University, respectively. She's passionate about design, plants, entrepreneurship, and books (especially old ones). Her other published work includes *The Ancient Frankenstein*, and the novella *The Night Wheel*.

www.ingramcontent.com/pod-product-compliance
Lightning Source LLC
Chambersburg PA
CBHW030906080526
44589CB00010B/170